SHEFFIELD WEDNESDAY

A PICTORIAL HISTORY

JASON DICKINSON

AMBERLEY

ACKNOWLEDGEMENTS

Any publication requires the help, patience and expertise of countless individuals and organisations. I would therefore like to thank, in no particular order, the following, and apologise in advance for anyone I have omitted. Such a volume would not be possible without the help and patience of my wife Michelle, while the project would not have even reached publication stage without the staff at Amberley Publishing and especially Tom Furby.

Thanks to all at Sheffield Wednesday, especially Trevor Braithwait, and also special thanks to Lee Bullen for contributing the foreword. Also, thanks to staff at both the local studies and archive facilities in Sheffield, where I have spent far, far too many hours over the last twenty or so years. In addition, thanks to Mick Grayson, Craig Swift, Pete Law, John Brodie. Chris Edwards and Clive Nicholson for supplying various images, and a big thanks to club photographer Steve Ellis for permitting use of his excellent photographs.

Jason Dickinson

First published 2014

Amberley Publishing
The Hill, Stroud, Gloucestershire, GL5 4EP
www.amberley-books.com

Copyright © Jason Dickinson, 2014

The right of Jason Dickinson to be identified as the Author of this work has been asserted in accordance with the Copyrights, Designs and Patents Act 1988.

ISBN 978 1 4456 1950 7 (print)
ISBN 978 1 4456 1968 2 (ebook)

British Library Cataloguing in Publication Data.
A catalogue record for this book is available from the British Library.

Typesetting by Amberley Publishing.
Printed in Great Britain.

FOREWORD

In many respects, I have been lucky that my career in football has taken me all over the globe and exposed me to many different cultures, from the UK to Australia and from Hong Kong to Greece. At school, like the vast majority of my peers, I just wanted to be a professional footballer and spent countless hours on the playing fields of my hometown, with Scotland usually winning the World Cup and me grabbing the winner against, of course, England! Unfortunately, like the vast majority of football-mad kids, that dream did not quite go according to plan and I would not make the grade, firstly for being too small and then for not being strong enough. Therefore, by my late teens, I was working in an Edinburgh Building Society, while playing part-time in the lower reaches of the Scottish Leagues for the likes of Stenhousemuir, before dropping back into Scottish junior football.

It was at this point in my life, aged twenty-one, that I took the momentous decision to leave my life in Scotland behind and move to Australia on a one-year visa. A mate of mine was already over there and with his help I would spend an enjoyable twelve months 'Down Under', where my goalscoring form – I played the vast majority of my career as a striker – alerted scouts. I was offered, and signed, my first ever full-time professional playing contract, at Hong Kong-based side Kui Tan. Moving to South East Asia was a real learning curve, from both a cultural and football perspective, but I had a terrific four years out there, even fulfilling my childhood wish of playing against England when I was picked for a representative side, although the prophecy of grabbing the winning goal did not come to fruition!

While I was abroad, I met and married an English girl, but a move to Greek football, in 1998, provided an altogether different challenge as, unlike both Australia and Asia, English was rarely spoken. To help my integration into the side, I started to learn Greek and I believe this was much appreciated by my new teammates – who incidentally included Dimitrios Konstantopoulos who played for Hartlepool United against the Owls in the 2005 play-off final, more of which later! My career subsequently turned full circle as a decade after being rejected, I returned home to sign a one-and-a-half-year deal with Dunfermline Athletic. This eventually stretched to almost four years, and it was during this time that I started to move back on the field of play, dropping initially to right-wing back, then to right-back and eventually finding a new home at centre-half. I helped The Pars reach the 2004 Scottish Cup final, but my farewell appearance would end in disappointment as Celtic won 3-1 at Hampden Park.

When I was signed by Chris Turner for Wednesday, in the summer of 2004, it was primarily as a right-back, although I thought my stay would probably only be the length of my initial one-year deal. My first senior game for the Owls proved somewhat disastrous, as visitors Colchester United scored three late goals to win at Hillsborough on the opening day of the season. The result was a shock to both fans and players, as the squad had enjoyed a great pre-season in Ibiza and it was not the start we were looking for! Thankfully, a midweek win at Blackpool got the season up and running, although a relatively poor beginning meant I was playing under a new boss within a few weeks, Paul Sturrock taking over from Chris Turner.

The season, of course, ended on that unforgettable day in Cardiff, where I had the greatest pleasure to captain Wednesday on one of the best days in their modern history. The fact I lifted the play-off trophy, as team captain, made the day even more memorable from a personal point of view. Recollections from that day are still vivid: time standing still as youngster Drew Talbot netted a last-gasp fourth goal; the players doing the conga on the gridlocked motorway on the way home; and even my threesome in bed that night with my missus and the play-off trophy! By this time I was established in central defence, although I did earn a reputation as a utility player by appearing in every position on the field for the Owls – the set completed in February 2006 in a controversial game against relegation rivals Millwall. I don't know what was rarer that day, my clean sheet between the sticks – after replacing the injured David Lucas – or Frankie Simek's goal, but it helped Wednesday gain the much-needed three points! A flirt with the plays-offs followed, under another new manager, Brian Laws, and I had four great years in Sheffield, becoming versed in the 'Wednesday Way' of never taking the easy way when a harder route was available! My 148th, and final game, for Wednesday came in a crucial win at Leicester City in April 2008, but a hamstring injury meant I missed out on a farewell appearance, having to watch from the stands as Norwich City were beaten to preserve Championship status.

I left, having proven to myself I could hold my own in the second tier of English football, with many great memories, and it was back to Scotland and Falkirk. I was disappointed when I wasn't 'stripped' for The Bairns' 2009 Scottish Cup final appearance, and soon after I joined the coaching staff, eventually becoming assistant to new manager Steven Pressley – I had started studying for my UEFA 'A' licence while at Wednesday. Unfortunately, stringent cost-cutting measures led to my departure from the club. I was now amicably divorced from my wife and living in Scotland with my Sheffield-born girlfriend, but we were soon both back in the Steel City, agreeing to take over the estate agent business of my partner's parents, who had decided to retire. The plan was for us to both work full-time in the business, but you never know what is around the corner, and while doing some scouting for Watford, I was asked by Sean McAuley to help out at Wednesday's academy, purely on a part-time basis. The imminent introduction by the FA of the Elite Player Performance Plan subsequently opened up several new coaching roles, and suddenly I was back at Hillsborough on a full-time basis, with responsibility for the under-21 development side, as the club secured Category Two status.

I have loved playing and working at Sheffield Wednesday and was delighted to be offered a more senior coaching position this year, after assisting Stuart Gray at first team level, and have never considered leaving the club when various opportunities have arisen. I hope you enjoy reading this new history of one of England's oldest and greatest clubs and continue to show your loyalty in such great numbers.

Lee Bullen

THE EARLY YEARS

There is no doubt that without the game of cricket, the world-famous Sheffield Wednesday Football Club would not exist today. The Wednesday Cricket Club, formed in 1820, was one of hundreds of such clubs that were born in the early nineteenth century as the new summer game quickly gained popularity. It was the highly skilled workers of the town of Sheffield, often referred to as 'little mesters', who were the driving force behind the formation of the original cricket club, naming the team after their only half-day of the working week, which of course happened to be Wednesday! The Wednesday Cricket Club remained a competitive force on the Sheffield sporting scene during their formative years, while in the early 1850s a new Factory Law was passed, which meant a Saturday half-day for the vast majority of workers. This proved the catalyst for the emergence of another sport as Association football, which had started in its organised form in the public schools and universities, started to gain favour with the masses.

By the mid-1860s, the members of Wednesday Cricket Club had become restless that their sporting activities were restricted to just four summer months. Finally, in September 1867, it was decided to form an additional sporting branch, and the still relatively new pastime of Association football was the game in question. The city is, of course, the birthplace of the modern game, with both Sheffield FC and Hallam FC predating the world's oldest League club, Notts County. At the time, teams were being formed in every district of the city and interest was high, so after a notice was placed in the local press, a large and enthusiastic audience gathered on 4 September 1867 at the Adelphi Hotel (the site on which the modern-day Crucible Theatre stands). The sole aim was to form a football section that would keep the members together between the calendar months of September and April, and it was John Pashley who performed the first act in the long history of Sheffield Wednesday FC by proposing 'that a football club be formed in connection with the cricket club, and that no body of persons shall be empowered to sever the two clubs without the unanimous consent of a general meeting, six days' notice to be given to every member of the two clubs'. The motion was seconded by William Littlehales, with financial agent Ben Chatterton elected the first president and John Marsh as secretary and playing captain, and the colours of blue and white were chosen – the story had begun.

The club quickly secured a playing pitch in the Highfields district of Sheffield, just off modern-day London Road, and the first recorded fixture was played in early October 1867 when the members held an inter-club game. A week later, the Wednesday FC got off to a winning start when they triumphed at Norfolk Park, and that inaugural season saw the fledgling club play a series of 'challenge matches' against the likes of Heeley, Dronfield and Broomhall. Their first piece of silverware was also quickly secured – in February 1868 – as Oliver Cromwell, manager of the Theatre Royal in Sheffield, offered a fine silver cup for a competition for clubs less than a year old. Four teams entered and it was Wednesday who won the Cromwell Cup at the Bramall Lane final, beating Garrick 1-0 in extra time. Captain Marsh was chaired off the pitch at the conclusion, and a fine, 600-strong crowd had proven that there was certainly an appetite for the sport in Sheffield. The cup competition grabbed the interest of the local media, but in the late 1860s little else was reported about the new game, and it would not be until the dawn of the new decade that the local press began to report football in any depth. During the 1870s, Wednesday moved grounds to Myrtle Road, Heeley, and started to emerge as a dominant force in the town, facing such 'foreign' opposition as Derby Derwent and Nottingham Castle before travelling out of England for the first time to face Scottish side Clydesdale in April 1876.

The introduction of the FA Cup in 1871 had provided further impetus for the game, and the arrival of the Sheffield Challenge Cup, five years later, would boost the profile of Wednesday considerably. They took part in the first-ever game in the new competition and were the inaugural winners, beating Heeley in an amazing final that saw Wednesday recover from a three-goal deficit to snatch a dramatic 4-3 win. The cup was retained in 1878, while another ground move had seen the club sign a tenancy for the Sheaf House grounds, situated in the shadow of Yorkshire County Cricket's Bramall Lane home. Most of Wednesday's major home games still took place at Bramall Lane, however. Glasgow Rangers played only their second game outside of Scotland when they travelled to Sheffield in February 1878. A bumper crowd of 3,000 watched Wednesday win the inaugural final of the Wharncliffe Charity Cup in 1879, and a year later it was the FA Cup's turn to take centre stage as the club entered for the first time. That first season in the national competition helped take the name of Wednesday to a much wider audience, when hot favourites Blackburn Rovers were thrashed 4-0 in the opening game before the club eventually bowed out at the fourth-round stage, losing at Darwen. Wednesday reached the last four a year later where Blackburn Rovers gained revenge by winning 5-1 in the replayed semi-final. Another splendid run took them to the last sixteen in the following season, earning the club a national reputation as Cup fighters of some repute.

The progress of the football section led to the summer and winter sports officially splitting into separate entities in 1883. Unfortunately for the latter, all the progress of the early 1880s quickly ebbed away as the decade passed with early exits in national and local cup competitions, encouraging other sides to challenge them as top dogs in the town of Sheffield. This situation was exacerbated in 1886 when internal problems meant that the club failed to apply in sufficient time to enter that season's FA Cup competition, and were forced to watch on as the likes Sheffield works team Lockwood Brothers (significantly including Wednesday stalwarts Tom Cawley and Billy Mosforth) enjoyed a notable run to the latter stages, beating Nottingham Forest en route. The success of the new club proved a catalyst for change, as the spring of 1887 would prove to be pivotal in the history of Wednesday.

PROFESSIONALISM &
LEAGUE FOOTBALL

The issue of professionalism had slowly grown in significance in the 1880s, as teams from across the Pennines embraced the new ethos and started to challenge the old order of amateur teams comprised of 'gentlemen' players. In the mid-1870s, Wednesday had brought highly rated footballer James Lang across the Scottish border to supposedly work for a club official, but he

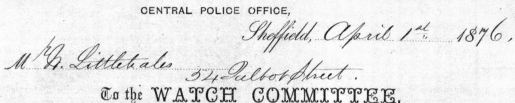

CENTRAL POLICE OFFICE,

Sheffield, *April 1st 1876.*

Mr G. Littlehales
54 Fulton Street.

To the WATCH COMMITTEE.

MAY BE PAID AT THE POLICE OFFICE FROM NINE TO TWO, AND FROM FIVE TO EIGHT, EVERY DAY.

1876				
Mch 18	To attendance of 2 PCs at Bramall Lane Grounds 2 hours @ 1/6 each		3/-	
17	To Same 6 PC		12/-	
			15/-	

Received 15/-
April 21/76

Jno Jilley
Supt

Above: A receipt for policing costs for a 1876 game at Bramall Lane.

Far left: The Wednesday Athletic Sports Day Trophy, 1873.

Left: Muscroft's winner's medal from the 1877 Sheffield Challenge Cup.

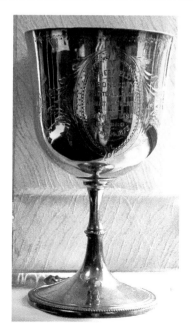

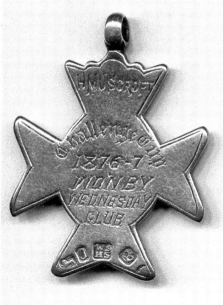

spent most of his days reading the newspapers and drinking tea! However, despite this nod to professionalism, the Wednesday hierarchy still steadfastly refused the 'evil' of paying players, and this stance came to a dramatic conclusion in April 1887, when prominent Wednesday players were instrumental in forming a side called Sheffield Rovers, who subsequently played the requisite two games to gain entry into the FA Cup for the 1887/88 season. Two meetings then decided the future of Wednesday, with the first, held by Sheffield Rovers, seeing Tom Cawley propose that the old club be given one last chance to adopt professionalism. The motion was carried and, at a special meeting of the Wednesday FC, the players virtually demanded that the club shake off their amateur roots and embrace the new era or they would, en masse, switch their allegiance to Sheffield Rovers. The club officials really did not have any choice in the matter, as to turn down the request would almost certainly have signalled the end of Wednesday as a dominant force on the Sheffield football scene. It was agreed to pay 6s for home games and 7s 6d for away games – the next chapter in the club's history had begun.

The professional era had dawned but Wednesday officials knew that they needed a new home, as Bramall Lane took a sizeable cut from all big games staged there and it was difficult to collect admission monies at Hunters Bar, where they had moved in around 1882. Therefore, in the summer of 1887, the club signed a seven-year lease with the Duke of Norfolk for a plot of swampy land just off Queen's Road. This was duly named Olive Grove, the club's first fully enclosed and permanent home ground. The princely sum of £5,000 was spent to bring the ground up to standard and Blackburn Rovers provided the opposition when a 4-4 draw officially opened the new enclosure in September 1887. A crowd of around 2,000 attended that inaugural game and, over the next few seasons, crowd levels slowly increased, with players such as Billy Mosforth, who was christened 'little wonder', proving an early hero to that first generation of Wednesday supporters. The formation of the Football League in 1888 saw the next major change in the English game unfold, although Wednesday initially failed to gain admission to the competition, which consisted mainly of clubs from Lancashire. The huge success of that first season of League football showed that regular scheduled home and away games were certainly the future – fans were getting tired of friendly and minor cup fixtures – and in 1889, Wednesday were founder members of the Football Alliance League (FAL), with club official John Holmes appointed as president of the new competition. That first season proved hugely successful for Wednesday as they not only walked away with the League title but also reached the FA Cup final for the first time, beating Football League clubs Accrington, Notts County and Bolton Wanderers to set up a Kennington Oval clash with old enemy Blackburn Rovers. The final proved a bridge too far for non-League Wednesday and they crashed 6-1, Mickey Bennett netting the consolation goal, but it was a season of real progress and crowds at Olive Grove continued to rise. This was the case in the 1890/91 season, but incredibly Wednesday went from prince to pauper by ending the season with the wooden spoon, much to the surprise of all concerned! Two notable games did take place: Wednesday and United met for the first time, the blue-and-whites winning 2-1 at Olive Grove; and Harry Woolhouse scored five goals as Lancashire club Halliwell were beaten 12-0 in the FA Cup – a result that still stands today as Wednesday's biggest-ever victory.

The Blades, as Wednesday were commonly called in those days, would spend one more season in the FAL, finishing fourth, before the Football League expanded to two divisions in 1892, with the rival League providing the majority of the clubs in the new second tier,

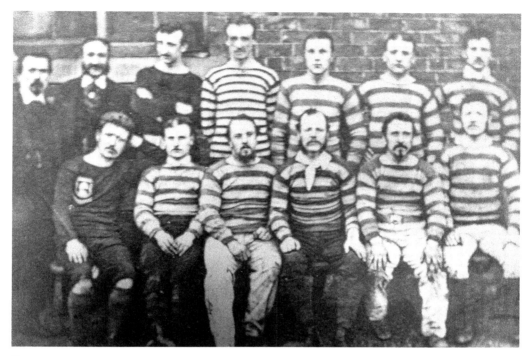

Team group, 1878.

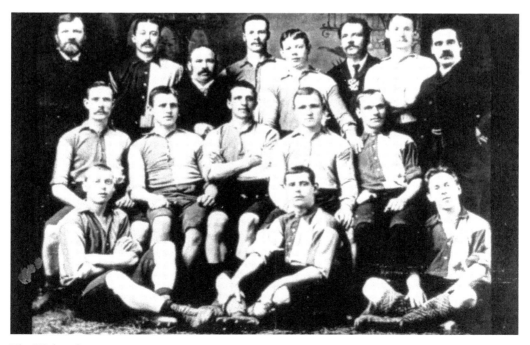

The Wednesday, 1890.

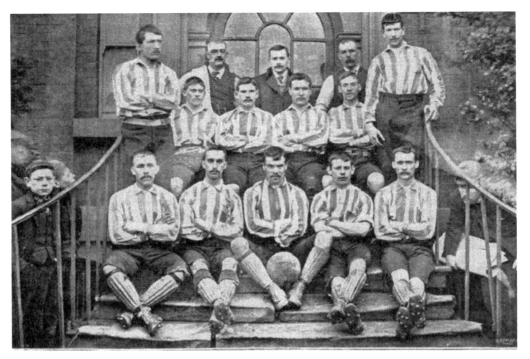

First season in the Football League, 1892/93.

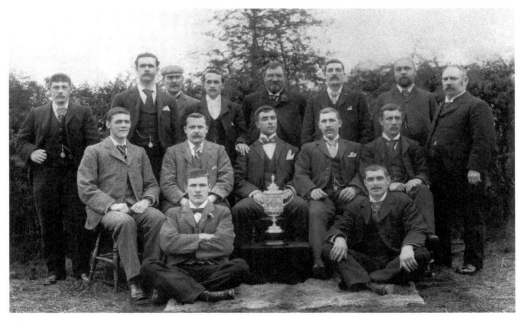

FA Cup winners for the first time, 1896.

although the stature of Wednesday meant that they were voted straight into the First Division. Plans were therefore made for the arrival of League soccer, with Olive Grove spruced up and several new signings made, including Alec Brady, Harry Davis and Sandy Rowan. Key players Fred Spiksley – nicknamed 'The Olive Grove Flyer' – captain Tom Brandon, 'keeper Bill Allan, old warhorse Billy Betts and Albert 'Clinks' Mumford completed the nucleus of the squad that would lead Wednesday into the uncharted territory of the Football League. A large travelling support swelled the attendance at Notts County's Castle Ground for the club's first-ever League fixture – the kick-off was delayed twenty-five minutes due to fans encroaching onto the playing surface. The game did eventually start and Wednesday's first goal in League soccer, scored by captain Tom Brandon after eleven minutes, proved decisive to give his side a perfect start to life in the new competition. Victory was also secured in the club's first-ever League home game – Accrington beaten 5-2 – and Wednesday enjoyed a great first half of the season, sitting third in early January 1893, before seven consecutive losses pushed them down to a final finishing position of twelfth. A win on the final day of the fixture list ensured the end-of-season 'test matches' – where teams from both divisions competed to either retain their top-flight place or earn promotion to the first tier – were avoided. Winger Fred Spiksley finished that first-ever season as top goalscorer with sixteen in League and Cup football, while almost 150,000 fans came through the Olive Grove turnstiles, giving an average of just under 10,000. These figures proved that the arrival of League football had been fully embraced by the club's fans; the aggregate admissions were almost double those recorded in the final season in non-League football!

FA CUP GLORY

The highlight of the 1893/94 season was a run to the last four of the FA Cup, losing to Bolton Wanderers at Fallowfield, Manchester. The League campaign was almost a mirror image of the previous season as Wednesday started badly but finished strongly to record another twelfth-placed finish. Fred Spiksley was again top scorer with sixteen goals in competitive matches. Attacker Alec Brady became the first Wednesday player to score a League hat-trick, against Derby County in October 1893, while three League games were all abandoned within a six-week period to snow, rain and fog as the English winter decimated the fixture list.

Another semi-final appearance in the 'English Cup' again captured the imagination of the fans in the following season, with an estimated 28,000 supporters packing Olive Grove to the rafters for the quarter-final win over Everton. Unfortunately, the run ended against West Bromwich Albion, but Wednesday had certainly restored their reputation as a club to be feared in the blue ribbon event of the English football calendar. After two near misses in the FA Cup, the 1895/96 season finally provided the glory the club had craved. A terrific run in the competition took them to the final, where they overcame Wolverhampton Wanderers to bring the trophy back to Sheffield for the first time. A side containing the likes of England international Tommy Crawshaw, club captain Jack Earp, Ambrose Langley and Bob Ferrier started their run with a win at non-League Southampton St Marys in January 1896, and they subsequently overcame Sunderland and Everton before defeating Bolton Wanderers in a replayed semi-final at Trent Bridge. Wednesday fans therefore travelled in numbers to Crystal Palace for the final, swelling the crowd to over 48,000, and were celebrating just after kick-off when club legend Fred Spiksley put his side ahead. The Black Country side soon levelled, but Spiksley struck again to secure the trophy, collected by proud captain Earp, and celebrations began in earnest back in Sheffield. When the team returned home with the cup, the streets of the city were packed with fans and the planned route, on horse-drawn carriage, had to be abandoned partway through due to the sheer volume of well-wishers wanting to see their heroes and catch a glimpse of the famous trophy.

Those scenes of jubilation would contrast greatly with the club's fortunes at the end of the nineteenth century as, despite posting consecutive top-six finishes in the First Division in 1897 and 1898, the club once again found its very future in doubt as relegation was suffered and the expansion of the railway network meant the sad loss of Olive Grove to the development. Rumours regarding their recently upgraded home first surfaced just after the FA Cup triumph, but fears were allayed when it was confirmed that the vast majority of the land was owned by the Sheffield Corporation (the modern-day city council). However, in the summer of 1898, it emerged that the land would, after all, be needed for the expansion of the Northern Line, and Wednesday were given notice to leave by September 1898. The club was given grace to complete the season, but it was against this backdrop that Wednesday endured a torturous season, winning only eight games to finish rock bottom in the First Division. During the campaign, a plan to move back to the Sheaf House grounds was abandoned, and the club subsequently held a ballot to gauge the opinion of supporters. A move to Carbrook emerged as a favourite, with Owlerton – a venue not even reached by the tram network at that point – as second choice. The news that all fans had been waiting for finally broke just nine days before the last-ever game at Olive Grove, when club president John Holmes announced there would be a new share issue, which it was hoped would raise £5,000; the reason being the committee had decided the long-term future of the club would be best suited by relocation to the green meadowland of High Bridge, Owlerton, on the north side of the River Don. In hindsight, the decision was a bold move by the club hierarchy, but within a short space of time, the transport links to the area vastly improved and the traditional heartland of Wednesday fans slowly moved from central Sheffield to the north of the city.

The summer of 1899 also saw a significant change in the legal status of the football club, as Wednesday were converted into a Limited Company, and George Senior appointed the first chairman on a board of directors that contained newly appointed secretary Arthur Dickinson and twenty other directors. The stated aim of the new company was to 'acquire freehold estate in the parish of Ecclesfield and to promote the practice and play of football, cricket, tennis, cycling and other sports'.

The purchase of Owlerton, from famous Sheffield Silversmith James Dixon's, was duly completed and work started in a furious bid to turn the green field into a football ground fit to host League soccer. The old stand at Olive Grove was moved, brick by brick, and reassembled on the river side of the ground, with railings and turnstiles installed in readiness for the opening game.

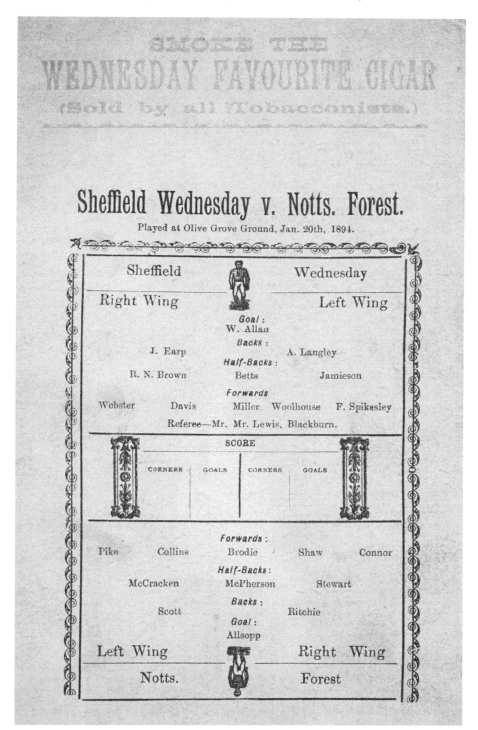

SMOKE THE
WEDNESDAY FAVOURITE CIGAR
(Sold by all Tobacconists.)

Sheffield Wednesday v. Notts. Forest.

Played at Olive Grove Ground, Jan. 20th, 1894.

Sheffield   Wednesday

Right Wing   Left Wing

Goal :
W. Allan

Backs :
J. Earp   A. Langley

Half-Backs :
R. N. Brown   Betts   Jamieson

Forwards
Webster   Davis   Miller   Woolhouse   F. Spikesley

Referee—Mr. Mr. Lewis, Blackburn.

SCORE

CORNERS	GOALS	CORNERS	GOALS

Forwards :
Pike   Collins   Brodie   Shaw   Connor

Half-Backs :
McCracken   McPherson   Stewart

Backs :
Scott   Ritchie

Goal :
Allsopp

Left Wing   Right Wing

Notts.   Forest

A 1894 match card *v.* Nottingham Forest.

OWLERTON & THREE TITLES

Any concerns about moving the club out of the city centre were quickly allayed on the opening day of the 1899/1900 season, when around 12,000 enthusiastic fans packed into the new ground to see neighbours Chesterfield visit for a Second Division fixture. Wednesday got off to a perfect start in their new surroundings, beating their Derbyshire visitors 5-1, and it would not be until the two teams met again, on 30 December, that defeat was tasted for the first time. In fact, Wednesday ended the season with a 100 per cent home success record (one of only six teams to achieve this feat in English League football) and finished two points clear of Bolton Wanderers to secure the Second Division championship. New signing Jocky Wright topped the scorers list with twenty-five from thirty-three League games, while defensive rocks Tommy Crawshaw and Herod Ruddlesdin kept the opposition out at the other end of the pitch. The season was also remembered for a bad-tempered FA Cup tie against Sheffield United, who at the time were reigning League champions. The first tie was abandoned due to a snowstorm at Bramall Lane, and the teams then drew to force an Owlerton replay. Over 83,000 fans watched the three games, and the final match turned into somewhat of a 'kicking match' as Wednesday lost 2-0 and ended the game with nine men after two players were sent from the field for rather 'overenthusiastic' challenges!

After regaining their top-flight place at the first attempt, Wednesday broke the club record transfer fee to pay £200 (approximately £22,000 today) for inside-forward Andrew Wilson. However, the large fee proved to be money well spent, and the Scot would provide invaluable service as in twenty years at Wednesday, he would set records for both goals and appearances that have never been bettered. A record run of nineteen consecutive home wins came to an end when Preston North End won at Owlerton in October 1900. The club consolidated back in the top flight, finishing in mid-table despite failing to win a single game away from home. Victory at Liverpool, in October 1901, ended that long run without an away success, but despite finishing in mid-table again, two consecutive early exits in the FA Cup resulted in a few murmurs of discontent among shareholders and supporters. However, this was soon forgotten as Wednesday opened the 1902/03 campaign with a 3-2 win at Bramall Lane, and would challenge for the League title from that point onwards. A home win over Aston Villa, on New Year's Day, lifted Wednesday into the top two and despite another early Cup exit, their League form remained consistent and the top spot was secured in mid-March. Main rivals for the title were Sunderland, and when Wednesday finished their fixtures, beating West Bromwich Albion 3-1 at Owlerton, they held a single-point lead over the Wearsiders, who still had one game to play. That crucial fixture was against their fierce rivals Newcastle United. Wednesday were contesting the Plymouth Bowl against Notts County in the Devon town when news filtered through that the Geordies had, in fact, won 1-0, and Wednesday FC were champions of England! A reserve game was also being played at Owlerton on the same day and, when the news reached the crowd, the match was held up for several minutes as all concerned celebrated the huge achievement. When the team returned from their tour of the South West, they were welcomed into Midland station by the Sheffield Recreation Band – who provided music at home matches – and driven through the streets of the city before enjoying a 'slap-up' meal and then a night at the theatre. The definite key to the success was a settled side,

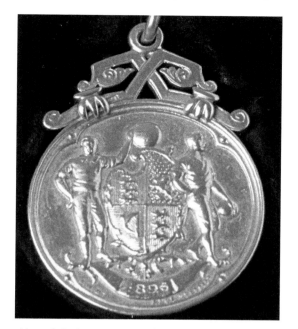

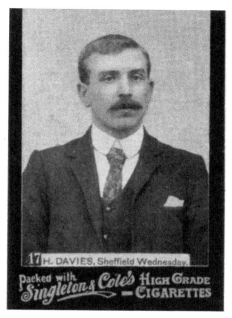

Above left: Tommy Crawshaw's winner's medal from the '96 final.

Above right: Harry Davis (1900–07), 67 goals in 235 games.

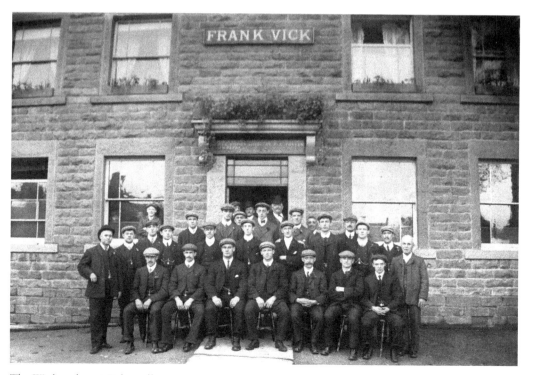

The Wednesday at Bakewell, *c.* 1900s.

as ten players missed a total of only twelve League games between them in the whole season, with Andrew Wilson, Ambrose Langley and Herod Ruddlesdin ever-present, and Tommy Crawshaw, Bob Ferrier, Jack Lyall and Jock Malloch missing only one game. Top scorer was Harry Davis with thirteen League goals, while the club fired championship medals during the summer and gave permission for a gala to be held at their ground, with the proviso that the elephants should be kept off the pitch!

It is always more difficult to defend a trophy but Wednesday started the 1903/04 season in great form, winning their opening three League fixtures to quickly top the table. They would remain in the top four positions for the whole of the season, and when the two Sheffield sides met on Boxing Day, Wednesday sat in second position behind United in first place – the only time this has occurred. The derby game finished all square and, by the end of January, Wednesday had regained top spot and remained there until a shocking 4-0 loss at Newcastle United, in the penultimate away game, allowed title rivals Manchester City to sneak past. A 4-2 win over Aston Villa a week later ensured that Wednesday ended their home programme unbeaten and meant they regained top spot, with their Manchester rivals set to play their final game midweek. In a rerun of the previous season, Wednesday would again secure the title without playing as it was Everton who did them a favour this time, beating City at Goodison Park to ensure the championship trophy remained in Sheffield. Victory in their last game put the gloss on another terrific season, while Goodison Park and Manchester City also featured in the club's FA Cup run – Sheffield Wednesday lost 3-0 to Machester City at Goodison Park in the semi-finals. The famous 'three Ls' back line of Lyall, Layton and Langley again kept the opposition out, while rapidly emerging forward Harry Chapman (brother of legendary Arsenal manager Herbert) grabbed sixteen goals to become a new darling of the Owlerton faithful.

Wednesday looked set to become the first English club to win a hat-trick of League titles when they reeled off seven straight victories, scoring twenty times, at the start of the following season. However, the wheels then fell off the juggernaut and they would only win another seven matches in the remainder of the season, to slip down to a disappointing mid-table position. One game of note was one of those winless matches, which must have actually felt like a victory, when Wednesday recovered from a 5-1 half-time deficit at home to Everton to snatch a last-minute equaliser in the only 5-5 draw in the history of the club. Wednesday were back on form in the FA Cup, and wins over Blackburn Rovers, Portsmouth and Preston North End set up a semi-final meeting with Newcastle United at Hyde Road, Manchester. Around 40,000 packed into the ground, but a single first-half goal was enough to send United to the final and leave Wednesday to play out a low-key end to the season. The club reached the last eight of the competition in 1906, losing at Everton. It was a much better season in the League, Wednesday leading the table for several weeks in the autumn before falling away over the Christmas and New Year period. Exciting recruit from the North East Jimmy Stewart became the first man to net twenty League goals in a top-flight campaign for the club, and he inspired a late run of form that lifted his side into a very satisfying third-place finish.

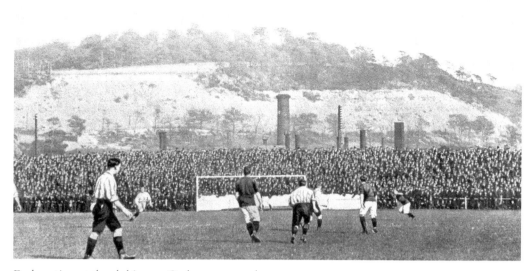

Early action at the club's new Owlerton ground.

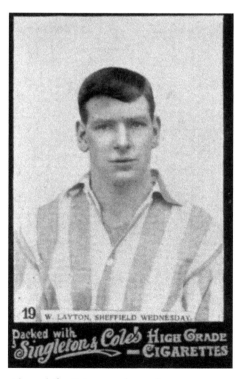

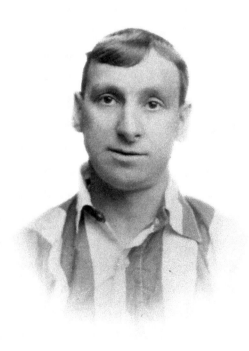

Above left: Baines trade card, 1900s.

Above right: Harry Chapman (1901–11), 100 goals in 299 games.

FA CUP – GLORY AND CALAMITY

Six wins from the opening nine League games of the 1906/07 season quickly put the club among the front runners, and they remained in contention until a run in the FA Cup took centre stage. Wednesday marched to the final, beating Wolverhampton Wanderers (3-2), Southampton (3-1 in a replay), Sunderland (1-0 in a replay) and Liverpool (1-0) to set up a semi-final meeting with Woolwich Arsenal at St Andrews, Birmingham. A double from Andrew Wilson and a goal from Jimmy Stewart led their side to a 3-1 win over the Londoners, and the 'northern hordes' had another day in the capital to look forward to. Opponents were regular foes Everton (Wednesday have played more FA Cup ties against the Merseyside club than any other), and 84,584 fans filled the Crystal Palace ground (a ground not connected to the football club of the same name) to watch the blue ribbon event of the English sporting calendar. It was the fans travelling back to Yorkshire who would be celebrating on 20 April 1907, as goals from Jimmy Stewart and winger George Simpson secured a 2-1 success and led to Sheffield-born captain Tommy Crawshaw lifting the famous 'tin pot' aloft to the acclaim of the travelling Wednesday fans.

The club's record in the FA Cup following that win couldn't have been more different with Wednesday falling to several embarrassing exits, including a few to non-League opposition. This terrible run started with the defence of the trophy. Around 500 Owls fans travelled all the way to deepest Norfolk to see non-League Norwich City send their side tumbling out of the competition at their old Newmarket Road ground. Just over a year later, Second Division minnows Glossop North End knocked Wednesday out at Owlerton. Southern League Northampton Town and Coventry City then completed a four-year run of Cup heartache. Away from the glamour of the FA Cup, Wednesday remained a competitive force in the top flight, finishing in the top six in four seasons out of five between 1908 and 1912. Meanwhile, the side was slowly evolving, with star man Jimmy Stewart leaving for new pastures and Wednesday breaking the club transfer record to buy Scottish attacker David McLean for the princely sum of £1,000. In his first season at Wednesday, McLean broke the club record by grabbing twenty-five top-flight goals (including four in a 8-0 home win over Sunderland on Boxing Day 1911), and in a dramatic 1912/13 season he bagged an incredible thirty League goals in just thirty-six appearances. That season was full of incident as it not only included the club's highest-ever League defeat – 10-0 at Aston Villa – but also saw Wednesday agonisingly close to a third League title as a terrific run of five straight wins left them top of the table with just four games remaining. Unfortunately, only one further win was accrued and they slipped to a disappointing third-place finish. The season was also notable for the gift of a wooden Owl, by player George Robertson in October 1912, which was subsequently placed under the North Stand. A run of four consecutive home wins duly occurred and, despite the club stating their nickname would remain the 'Blades', it was too late and from that point on the club became known as the 'Owls'.

The following season saw major development work at Owlerton – it would be many years before it was commonly referred to as Hillsborough, despite the club adopting the name – with an ambitious plan to replace the old Olive Grove Stand with a state-of-the-art structure. The services of famous football ground architect Archie Leach were procured and, by the autumn of 1913, the hugely impressive new structure was opened to the public, initially without a

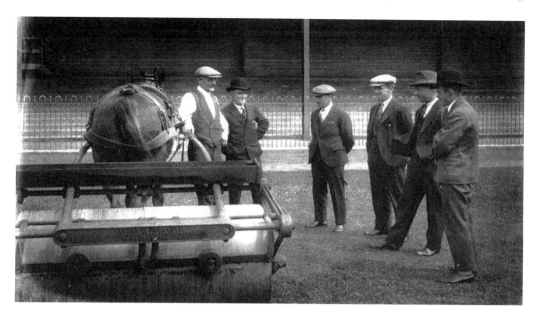

Above: An old-style lawnmower.

Right: The Wednesday penny handbook, 1901.

Sheffield Wednesday Football Album

PRICE ONE PENNY.

BEER FROM MALT AND HOPS ONLY.

Carter, Milner, & Bird, Limited,

HOPE BREWERY,

. . MOWBRAY STREET, SHEFFIELD. . .

Telephone 2578.

Beg to inform the Public at large and the Trade generally that they brew all their Noted Ales and Beers from

MALT AND HOPS ONLY,

and give a Printed Warranty to that effect on every Cask sent out, and have done so for years. Copies of Analysts' Reports re our produce are given below. The originals of these Certificates can be seen at the Registered Office of the Company, Mowbray Street.

(Signed) CARTER, MILNER, & BIRD, LTD. G. BIRD, Secretary.

CERTIFICATES OF ANALYSTS.

The Laboratory, 16 and 17, Devonshire Square, Bishopsgate,
London, E.C., December 5th, 1900.

I hereby certify that I have examined five samples of Beers supplied by Messrs. CARTER, MILNER, AND BIRD, LIMITED, HOPE BREWERY, SHEF-FIELD, and, as the result of exhaustive Analyses, find them to be of SUPERIOR QUALITY, PERFECTLY PURE AND WHOLESOME, and BREWED FROM MALT AND HOPS ONLY. They are absolutely free from Arsenic or any other irritant poison or deleterious impurity.

I have also Examined the Brewing Records and find that no glucose, invert sugar, or any other substitute for malt is employed in the production of these beers.

(Signed) MATTHEW J. CANNON, F.C.S.

Laboratory, 12, Lombard Street, Newcastle-on-Tyne, December 6th, 1900.

Report on Five Samples of Beer received from Messrs. CARTER, MILNER, AND BIRD, LIMITED, HOPE BREWERY, SHEFFIELD, and marked, X., XX., XXX., XXXX., XXXXX. respectively.

REPORT.—THESE BEERS ARE BREWED FROM MALT AND HOPS ONLY. I have carefully tested them for harmful and poisonous ingredients, and find them ABSOLUTELY FREE. They are, in all respects, PURE. AND WHOLESOME, (Signed) W. H. BLAKE, F.C.S.

J. Whitham, Printer, 18, Vincent Road, Sheffield.

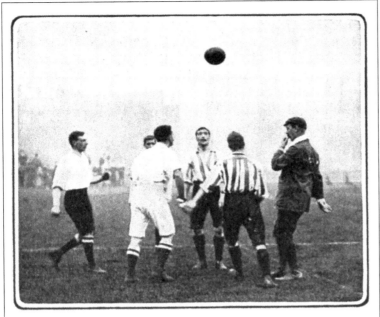

THE CORINTHIANS v. SHEFFIELD WEDNESDAY

A throw-up by the referee

Left: A 1902 friendly *v.* The Corinthians.

Below left: Champions of England – 1902/03.

Below right: Tribute to 'keeper Jack Lyall.

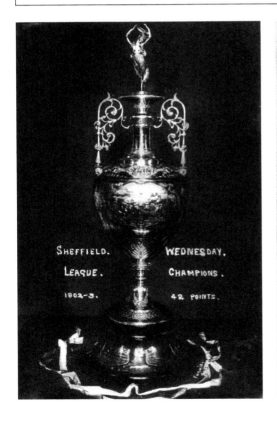

SHEFFIELD. WEDNESDAY.
LEAGUE. CHAMPIONS.
1902-3. 42 POINTS.

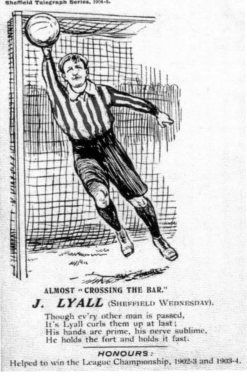

Sheffield Telegraph Series. 1904-5.

ALMOST "CROSSING THE BAR."
J. LYALL (SHEFFIELD WEDNESDAY).

Though ev'ry other man is passed,
It's Lyall curls them up at last;
His hands are prime, his nerve sublime,
He holds the fort and holds it fast.

HONOURS :
Helped to win the League Championship, 1902-3 and 1903-4.

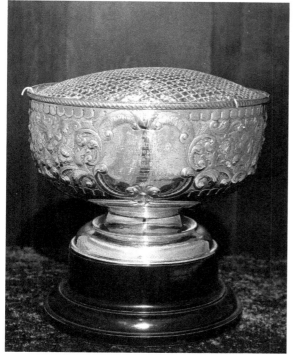

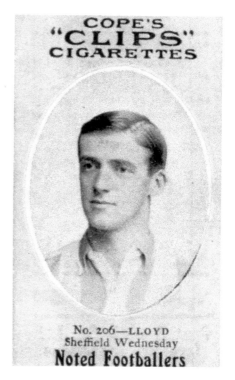

Above left: The Plymouth Bowl.

Above right: Billy Lloyd (1906–12), 7 goals in 84 games.

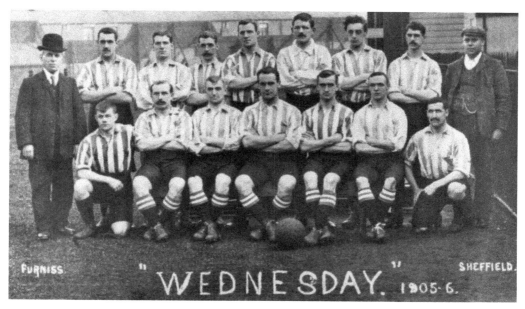

Team group, 1905/06.

roof! When finished, the stand was rated as the finest in English football and Wednesday fans clamoured to sit in the 'swell' new construction. The new stand was packed to the rafters in March 1914 when just under 57,000 fans watched Wednesday tumble out of the FA Cup to Aston Villa at the quarter-final stage. The Cup run had helped Wednesday fans forget a poor season in the League with the club just finishing outside of the bottom two relegation places. A dispute with star forward David McLean was a key factor in that poor form, as his demands for a three-year contract (unheard of in those days) saw an impasse. This led to the Scot playing in his homeland for several months –for Forfar – before returning to the fold and inspiring the aforementioned Cup run. The 1914/15 season saw Wednesday again in contention for what proved to be the last championship of the pre-war era, and by mid-March they found themselves top of the table (helped by a 7-0 rout of Bolton Wanderers in which all the goals were scored by different players). David McLean was back to his prolific best, and the likes of Jimmy Spoors, legendary 'keeper Teddy Davison, Andrew Wilson and Teddy Glennon were at the top of their games. Unfortunately, only a couple of wins until the end of the season dashed hopes of the title, and Wednesday ended the campaign in a rather disappointing seventh position.

When domestic football was suspended in 1915 – due to the ongoing war – the Owls were a highly competitive force in English football, but the war years were not kind on the club's fortunes. When the 'people's game' returned in 1919, the Owls had lost several of their 'old guard' to retirement, and former player Vivian Simpson paying the ultimate price on the killing fields of mainland Europe. The Wednesday hierarchy actually voted to close down during the war years, but the general consensus among other teams was to continue, and it was therefore left to club stalwart Arthur Dickinson to keep Wednesday afloat on a shoestring budget and a scarcity of players. A ruling by the Football Association early in the conflict did help the situation, the governing body announcing all players would effectively be classed as amateurs – receiving no remuneration – and that they could appear for any side, at their convenience, without the need for registration. As expected, football took a back seat during the bloody conflict and crowds dwindled as the appetite for the game waned. Thanks to profits brought forward from pre-war years, Wednesday managed to absorb the financial losses during the war and did achieve some small success, winning the 1917/18 subsidiary tournament thanks to a double over neighbours United (Teddy Glennon scoring four in a 5-0 win at Bramall Lane) and a 6-2 home romp over Barnsley. During the conflict, soldiers in their khaki uniforms were a regular sight at football grounds all over the country – Wednesday and other clubs allowing the servicemen in for free – and if nothing else, the game gave those men a brief respite from the day-to-day life of a country at war.

The First World War officially ended in November 1918 with the signing of an Armistice agreement, and fans quickly flooded back to football – over 55,000 were present in Sheffield for the two derby clashes with the Blades over the Christmas period that immediately followed. The return of national football was greatly anticipated, but for fans of The Wednesday it would be a long and torturous 1919/20 season. An apparent over-reliance on pre-war players and several unsuccessful forays into the transfer market left the club at the wrong end of the First Division table for the entire season. Club legends Andrew Wilson, Tom Brittleton and David McLean would all appear in their final games for the club, and Wednesday used a club record of forty-one players in an unsuccessful attempt to find a winning formula. The final figures for the season made grim reading – the Owls recorded only seven wins, netted just twenty-eight

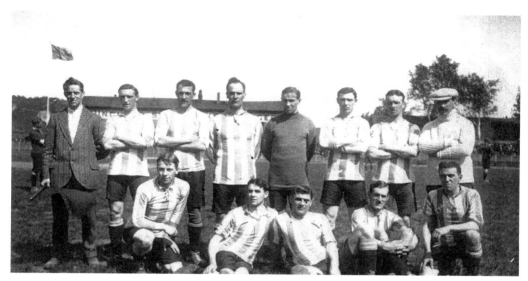

The Wednesday in Denmark, 1911.

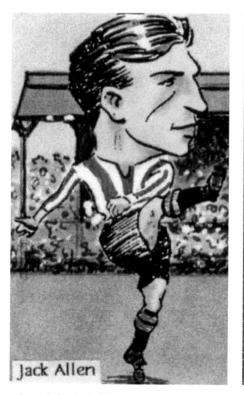

Jack Allen

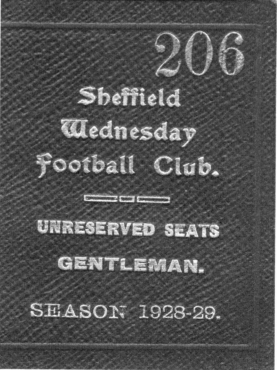

Above left: Jack Allen.

Above right: Season ticket for 1928/29 title-winning season.

goals and finished a staggering thirteen points adrift at the foot of the table. The biggest cull in club history duly occurred at the end of the campaign – a total of twenty-one players were either made available for transfer or not re-signed. At the club's Annual General Meeting it was announced that long-serving secretary-manager Arthur Dickinson, who had held the role for twenty-nine years, would be stepping down from his position. It would be a summer of change as the club restructured in an attempt to win back their treasured top-flight place.

BOB BROWN & PROMOTION

To usher in a new era, the club turned to their former North East scout, Bob Brown, who had been earning rave reviews while in charge at Southern League Portsmouth. The new man at the helm immediately brought former Hallam FC player Freddie Kean to Hillsborough, famously telling Kean at Portsmouth that the club were selling him and arriving in Sheffield in time to greet his new capture, much to Kean's surprise! After that disastrous first post-war season, Brown had no choice but to totally revamp his playing squad, quickly selling Jimmy Blair for a club record fee to Cardiff City. In the previous season, in a last-ditch attempt to avoid relegation, the club had signed former England captain George Wilson to set their own new transfer record, and the outstanding defender would captain Wednesday as they started the 1920/21 season with three consecutive 0-0 games. The first win under Brown came courtesy of a Johnny McIntyre strike at Stoke, but a lack of goals hindered any progress, with Wednesday netting only twenty goals in their first twenty-seven League games, McIntyre contributing the vast majority. This paucity in front of goal left the Owls on the fringes of the drop zone, but the signing of centre-forward Sam Taylor proved crucial. The club rallied to finish in a satisfactory tenth place, including a 6-0 win over Wolves. The top scorer was, unsurprisingly, McIntyre, with a highly impressive twenty-seven League goals, while the FA Cup showed it had lost none of its popularity – Wednesday set a new ground record when over 62,000 fans watched a replay loss to old foes Everton at Hillsborough.

Over the next four seasons, Brown slowly added players that would become club legends: men such as future England left-back Ernie Blenkinsop, centre-forward Jimmy Trotter and 'keeper Jack Brown. In the early throes of the 1921/22 campaign, a fall-out with prolific forward Johnny McIntyre led to his departure. The record attendance figure was smashed again in January 1923, when 66,103 packed into the ground to see the FA Cup tie with Barnsley. In the League, form was inconsistent and it would be fair to say that Wednesday never really challenged for promotion during the first five seasons of the Brown era, finishing just inside the top ten in four consecutive seasons before surprisingly slipping into the bottom half of the table in 1924/25. In hindsight, changes made in the summer of 1924 sowed the seeds of success, as new trainer Chris Craig joined the backroom staff and key man Billy Marsden signed from Sunderland, followed a few weeks later by Harold Hill. The month of September 1924 also saw the sad demise of the original Wednesday Cricket Club, mainly due to a dwindling membership. It would be almost ninety years before the club was reformed, in 2011, and regain its place on the Sheffield summer sporting map. Increasingly prolific centre-forward Jimmy Trotter also etched his name in the record books as he became the first player to score five times in a League fixture for Wednesday, achieving the feat in a December 1924 home game with Portsmouth. One surprise in the summer of 1925 was the decision of George Wilson to accept a transfer to Division Three (North) club Nelson – the offer of a dual playing/publican role being too good to turn down – and he would be absent when Bob Brown's new side finally gelled and took the Second Division by storm in 1925/26. The team that would lead the club to greater success in the late 1920s was starting to emerge as Wednesday won seven of their first ten League fixtures to settle into the divisional top two – Trotter netting four at home to Preston North End and then five against Stockport County! A treble from Harold Hill, in a 4-1 home win over Chelsea in late November, took Wednesday to the top of the table, and apart from one week when they dropped to third, the Owls remained in the promotion positions for the remainder of the campaign, being ably led by Sheffield-born captain Frank Froggatt (father of post-war player Redfern). Goals were not a problem – Wednesday scored eighty-eight in the League, with Trotter grabbing an astonishing thirty-seven in forty-one League appearances – and promotion was secured on the penultimate Saturday with a win at Southampton. A final-day home success over Blackpool clinched the Second Division title, and Wednesday fans looked forward with great anticipation after returning to what they believed was the club's rightful place in the top echelon of the English game.

THE GREAT ESCAPE BEFORE THE GOLDEN YEARS

A home defeat to Sheffield United opened the 1926/27 season, and Wednesday's defence managed to ship fifteen goals in the opening three games, including a 7-2 mauling at Tottenham Hotspur. Thankfully, clean sheets were then recorded in back-to-back home wins, and the season would prove to be one of high-scoring games combined with an excellent home record and dreadful away form. In fact, the Owls failed to register a single success on the road, gaining only six draws, while conversely winning all but half a dozen of their home matches. The incredible scoring form of Jimmy Trotter continued in the top division as he matched his feat of the previous season (thirty-seven goals in forty-one League matches) to win the proverbial 'golden boot' in England's showpiece division. If the club could improve that dire away record then hopes were high of a top-ten finish in the following season. The summer signings of Mark Hooper, Jack Allen, Jimmy Seed and Alf Strange seemed to strengthen that belief. It was, therefore, a shock to many when the season opened with a 4-0 defeat at Everton. Wednesday quickly slumped to the foot of the table, suffering defeat after defeat. Highlights were rare, with new signing Ted Harper becoming the only player in club history to score a hat-trick on his League debut at Derby County in November 1927. By the end of March 1928, supporters were resigned to relegation back to the Second Division as their side were seven points adrift at the foot of the table with only ten games remaining on the fixture list. What then took place was one of the most remarkable escapes from relegation in the history of the English game. Inspired by their new captain, former Spurs player Jimmy Seed, the Owls won eight of those final ten games to lift themselves to a final finishing position of fourteenth! The run commenced with a four-goal first-half salvo against Liverpool at Hillsborough and was quickly followed by a vital win at White Hart Lane – Seed netting one of the Wednesday goals in a 3-1 win. Victories against Tottenham (again), West Ham United, Portsmouth and Sunderland took the club into their final away game of the season at Highbury. The incredible run of form still left Wednesday bottom of the table, but a last-gasp goal from Seed at Arsenal lifted the Owls up to the dizzy heights of nineteenth, and victory over Aston Villa on the final afternoon completed the dramatic escape. The closest relegation scrap of all time finished with Tottenham (who had released Seed as they thought his best days had passed) drop into the bottom two for the only time in the season – shock news that eventually reached the North London club on a foreign tour as they had completed their fixtures early!

The momentum from that dramatic revival was carried into the new season as Wednesday quickly accumulated points, winning fourteen of their first twenty-one League games, including a 5-2 win over Sheffield United at Hillsborough. The Owls first hit top spot in November 1928, after a 3-2 home success over Liverpool. They remained in first place until the final home game of the season when they knew a win over Burnley would be enough to clinch a third First Division title. Over 33,000 were inside Hillsborough on that historic day and there was a hush when the Lancashire visitors took a first-half lead. However, Jack Allen's thirty-fifth goal of the season, just before the break, calmed any nerves, and although the game did finish all-square, it was time for celebration as the news came through that their title rivals, Leicester City, had also drawn, therefore handing the title to the blue-and-white wizards! It was their strong home record that secured the championship for the Owls – the side were unbeaten at Hillsborough, winning eighteen of twenty-one games, contrasting greatly with an away record that showed only three wins all season. Centre-forward Jack Allen was imperious in the famous No. 9 shirt, with legendary wingers Ellis Rimmer and Mark Hooper providing the ammunition, while captain Jimmy Seed, unrivalled England left-back Ernest Blenkinsop, Billy Marsden and 'keeper Jack Brown completed the nucleus of the title-winning side.

The old adage that you should strengthen from a position of power was embraced by Bob Brown as he added highly rated attacker Harry Burgess to the ranks in the summer of 1929. A momentous event then took place on 3 August as the club title was officially changed from Wednesday FC to Sheffield Wednesday FC. Wednesday started the new campaign with an emphatic 4-0 win at Portsmouth (two goals apiece from Rimmer and Allen) and quickly went top of the early League tables before Arsenal shocked the Hillsborough faithful by becoming the first team to lower the Owls' colours on their own ground since February 1928. However, this Wednesday side, without doubt the greatest in the club's history, would thereafter prove unstoppable, and Manchester United were thrashed 7-2 at Hillsborough before Wednesday reclaimed top spot as 1929 came to a close – a position they would not relinquish for the remainder of the season. The New Year started with a rip-roaring 3-3 draw against title rivals Manchester City. This outstanding side then roared away from the opposition to finish a mammoth ten points clear of Derby County, scoring a club record of 105 League goals, thirty-three notched by Jack Allen. The second half of the season included a 5-0 win at Grimsby Town, a 6-3 home success over challengers Derby County (a victory that retained the title with still four games to play), and a final-day 5-1 home win over Manchester City, with winger Mark Hooper netting three goals to finish the season in spectacular fashion. Such was the club's strength at that time that, in April 1930, four of the Owls' first-team regulars – Billy Marsden, Ernest Blenkinsop, Alf Strange and Mark Hooper – played for England against Scotland on the same day that Wednesday were on First Division duty at Liverpool, but the club just brought in a few reserves and duly won 3-1 at Anfield!

The Owls also came close to becoming the first team in the twentieth century to record the domestic double of League and FA Cup – in the latter they swept aside Burnley, Oldham Athletic, Bradford Park Avenue and Nottingham Forest to set up an Old Trafford clash with Yorkshire rivals Huddersfield Town in the last four. The semi-final tie proved highly controversial, mainly thanks to the performance of referee Mr Lewis, as Hooper put Wednesday ahead only for Town to level with a goal that was blatantly handled in the build-up. The West Yorkshire club then went back ahead before, in the last minute, a pass from Seed allowed Allen to fire home a deserved equaliser. However, as the players celebrated the official disallowed the goal, stating that he had blown the whistle for full-time just as the ball was about to cross the goal line!

A blow to the club's chances of recording a hat-trick of League tables came in May 1930, when star player Billy Marsden was seriously hurt while playing for England against Germany. It was only the skill of a German surgeon that saved his life, and although he recovered to play again, he never made another first-team appearance for the Owls. The Football Association paid Wednesday compensation, but this was scant consolation. The close season also saw the departure of prolific attacker Jimmy Trotter, who moved to Torquay United after netting an astonishing 114 goals in just 159 games for the Owls. The defence of the title commenced with a 2-1 home win over Newcastle United, but it was Arsenal who streaked away in the early League tables, the North London club also beating Wednesday at Stamford Bridge in the Charity Shield. However, the Owls made steady progress and, in late November/early December 1930, scored an incredible twenty-five goals in just four League games! The run started with a 5-2 win at Leicester City, before a Hooper treble helped the club thrash Blackpool 7-1 at Hillsborough. A 4-2 win on the South Coast at Portsmouth followed. Wednesday, rather fittingly, went back to the top of the League after recording the biggest League win in their entire history – 9-1 against Birmingham at Hillsborough (Hooper 3, Ball 2, Seed 2, Burgess and Rimmer). Wednesday and Arsenal traded places at the top of the table until late winter, but a run of only one win in six games, including a shock 5-1 reverse at Sunderland, firmly handed the initiative to the Gunners, and they took full advantage to strike a decisive blow in the title race, eventually finishing a full fourteen points clear of Wednesday, who ended the season down in third spot. The Owls again passed the century mark in League goals (102), although this looked almost shot shy when compared with Arsenal (127) and runners-up Aston Villa (128)! Top scorer was new No. 9 Jack Ball (twenty-nine goals in thirty-nine League and Cup games). Despite a record at Wednesday of eighty-five goals in just 114 games, previous centre-forward Jack Allen inexplicably found himself in the reserve side, before eventually moving to Newcastle United. One sad event during the season was the passing of former secretary Arthur Dickinson, who had joined the club's committee way back in 1876, and was effectively the pseudo team manager until tendering his resignation in the summer of 1920. The summer of 1931 also saw the departure of the vastly experienced and inspirational captain Jimmy Seed, who returned to London to take over as manager at Clapton Orient.

Despite failing to secure a hat-trick of League titles, Wednesday were still a major force in the English game, and they showed their intentions at the start of the 1931/32 season with an opening-day 6-1 win at Blackburn Rovers. This was quickly followed by a further fourteen goals in three more victories as Wednesday made a goal-laden 100 per cent start to the campaign. The Owls remained in the divisional top three throughout the first few months of the season, but a failure to win any of the final six games of the calendar year – including a 9-3 debacle at Everton where the legendary Dixie Dean helped himself to five goals – saw Wednesday tumble down into mid-table. A run to the last sixteen of the FA Cup then provided the impetus for League form, and seven wins in the final ten League games of the season pushed the club back into third place, a mere six points off champions Everton. In a true golden age of attacking football, Wednesday netted a mere ninety-six League goals, with Jack Ball topping the club's goalscoring chart with twenty-three top-flight strikes, although winger Ellis Rimmer equalled that tally thanks to two goals in the FA Cup.

In comparison to the previous seasons, Wednesday made an indifferent start to the 1932/33 season – sitting in mid-table in early October – but the old guard, mixed with new men such as Tony Leach, Ron Starling and Gavin Malloch, were still a force to be reckoned with, and Wednesday stormed back to again challenge for the title. However, with a fifth title within reach, the side then inexplicably lost form and recorded just one win in the final nine games of the campaign to post a third-place finish for the third season running. The shooting boots of Jack Ball were again prominent as he scored thirty-three in the First Division, and also set a club record when he netted ten times from the penalty spot – a record that would hold for almost fifty years.

FA CUP GLORY & RELEGATION

The remainder of the 1930s would be a story of great highs and disastrous lows: the club's greatest-ever manager, Bob Brown, departed; the FA Cup was lifted at Wembley; and the Owls tumbled out of the top flight. The resignation of Brown came early in the 1933/34 season as the loss of his wife just a few weeks earlier had left the popular manager a shadow of his former self. He was away from the club as the season started, effectively on compassionate leave and was then taken ill on his return to Hillsborough. It was not long before he retired, on health grounds, and handed the reigns to his assistant Joe McClelland. Off the field events clearly had an effect on the pitch and, by the time new manager Billy Walker had been appointed, the Owls had slid down to the fringes of the relegation places. The caretaker manager had actually been in charge for eleven games, during the club's search for Brown's successor, and it was a surprise to many when they appointed former England player Walker, who had no previous managerial experience and was still on the books as a player at Aston Villa – where he still holds the all-time record for goals. The new man did not immediately curry favour with Wednesday fans as one of his first acts was to sell prolific scorer Jack Ball to Manchester United; a deal that saw Neil Dewar travel in the opposite direction. The new boss did, however, quickly spark a revival, and Wednesday won the first four matches under his charge, dispelling any relegation worries. A run in the FA Cup created a new ground record at Hillsborough – 72,841 attended the 2-2 draw with Manchester City in the fifth round – while a 5-1 League defeat at Sheffield United had Wednesday fans sworn off bacon for several weeks! Unfortunately, the season also saw the sad passing of club trainer Chris Craig,

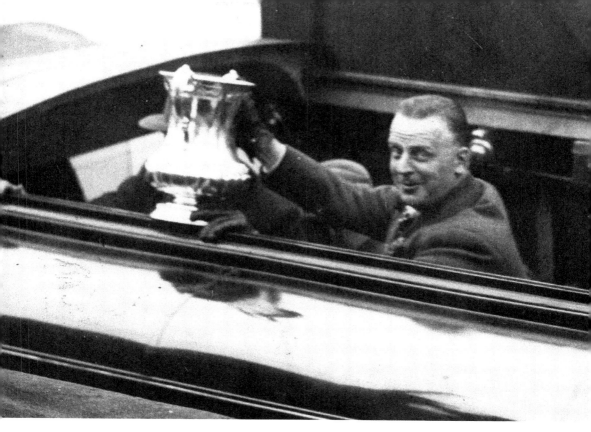

Above: Manager Billy Walker with the cup.

Right: Jack Brown at Wembley, 1935.

Below: Itinerary for 1936 tour of Denmark.

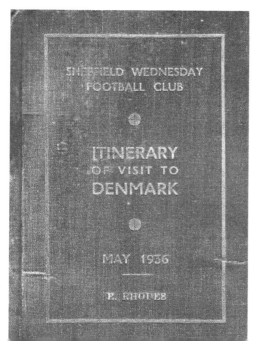

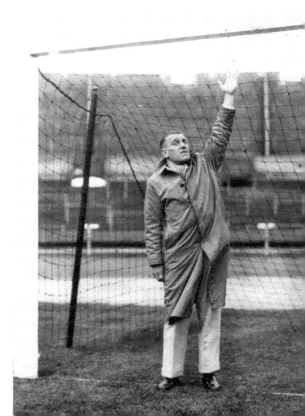

meaning that the two men behind back-to-back championship wins just a few years earlier were no longer at Wednesday.

The only new arrival of note in the following summer was full-back Joe Nibloe, but Walker's first full season in charge could be seen as nothing less than a huge success. Not only did he lead the club to another third-place finish in the First Division – remaining in the top half of the League table all season – but he also became one of only two Owls managers to oversee an FA Cup win, the other being Arthur Dickinson. A steady League campaign was quickly overshadowed as 1935 dawned with Cup wins over Oldham Athletic (3-1), Wolverhampton Wanderers (2-1) and Norwich City (1-0). A 1-0 win over Arsenal, in front of over 66,000 at Hillsborough, then set up a Villa Park clash with Burnley in the semi-final. A dominant display resulted in a comfortable 3-0 win over the Lancashire club – Rimmer (2) and Jack Palethorpe with the goals – and a first-ever visit for Wednesday to the Empire Wembley Stadium, which had opened in 1923, to face West Bromwich Albion in the FA Cup final. Thankfully, the Cup run did not adversely affect the club's League form, and Wednesday sat in fourth position in the First Division, with just two games remaining, when they travelled down to London for the showpiece final. Ironically, both Cup finalists shared a 1-1 draw from a rearranged League fixture at the Hawthorns just five days before the final, with highly rated and future Owls legend Jackie Robinson scoring on his debut for Wednesday. The final proved a thrilling affair, with Wednesday netting through Mark Hooper and Jack Palethorpe, and the match tied at 2-2 with just three minutes on the clock. It was then the turn of winger Ellis Rimmer to write his name into FA Cup folklore, becoming the first player to score in every round of the competition when he put the Owls ahead at the death. He put the 'icing on the cake' with a fourth for the Owls soon after and the estimated 10,000 travelling Wednesday fans could celebrate a third FA Cup triumph with gusto. It was left to captain Ronnie Starling to lift the famous old trophy and celebrations duly started back in Sheffield where the cup was paraded a week later, when Wednesday wrapped up their home campaign with a 1-0 win over Grimsby Town – Rimmer netting the solitary goal to take his seasonal total to twenty-six, a quite remarkable tally for a player who was an 'old fashioned' wing man.

It would be fair to say that the Cup win signalled the end of a golden period in the club's history, as an over-reliance on an ageing side and lack of investment from board level quickly saw Wednesday slump from a regular top-six position in the First Division down to the wrong end of the table. The 1935/36 season started brightly enough, including a Charity Shield win over Arsenal at Highbury, but three consecutive heavy defeats (conceding seventeen goals) in early autumn rocked the club and form never really recovered from that point onwards. This was not helped by the sale of FA Cup final scorer Palethorpe to Aston Villa, to the dismay of Owls fans. By early April, a 5-0 defeat at Middlesborough pushed the Owls into the relegation places and although Wednesday rallied to escape the drop, it was clear that the summer of 1936 would be a crucial one, with a major restructure required to arrest an alarming slump. Several new faces were brought into the club by Walker – the likes of Allenby Driver, Roy Smith and James McCambridge – but these proved not of the desired quality and Wednesday suffered a torrid season, despite a 6-4 home win over Everton in early September leaving them in mid-table. After Dewar's treble helped beat the Merseyside club, the Owls would win only seven more League games that season. Fans were again outraged when captain Ronnie Starling was sold to Aston Villa partway through the campaign. Relegation was confirmed with a heavy defeat at Manchester City on the penultimate Saturday of the season, a game

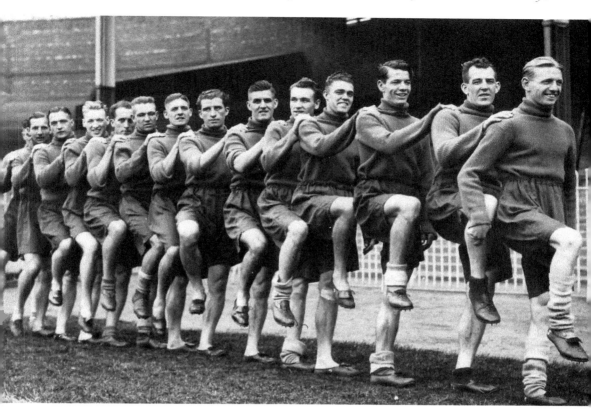

Above: Not quite the Moulin Rouge – 1930s training.

Below: Pre-season training, July 1937.

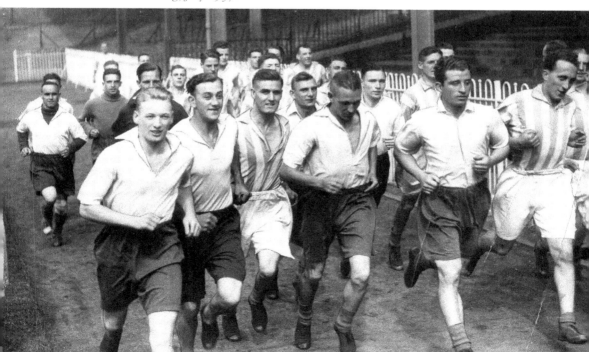

that saw the host team crowned as League champions. Their cross-city rivals, Manchester United, accompanied Wednesday down into the Second Division, and the pressure was now immense on both Walker and the Owls board to stop the rot and get the club back into the top flight as soon as possible.

STEEL CITY PROMOTION FIGHT

With the likes of Ellis Rimmer, Mark Hooper and Jack Brown at the end of their senior careers with the club, the Owls found themselves at a crossroads. The club hierarchy were again criticised in the summer of 1937 when published accounts showed a profit on the previous campaign, mainly due to a player trading surplus, which had seemingly weakened the playing staff. Sadly, there was little to brighten the gloom among Wednesday fans, as only minor investment in the side led to a dreadful start to life in the Second Division. The Owls won only two of their opening fourteen League games to slide to the bottom rung of the League ladder. It was perhaps symptomatic of the club at the time that the Owls gave a debut to Bob Curry (his only appearance) for the home game with Aston Villa, but inexplicably failed to register the player with the appropriate authorities. They were lucky to only receive a financial penalty and no points deduction. A shocking 4-1 defeat at neighbours Barnsley signalled the end for manager Walker, and he resigned twenty-four hours later, after attending a hostile shareholders' meeting. The club had just about hit rock bottom at this point, and it would be several weeks before a new manager would be installed, with the board of directors picking the team until the New Year. The new man at the helm was former Aston Villa boss Jimmy McMullan, who moved from Notts County to officially take over at Hillsborough in January 1938. He joined when Wednesday was still in the lower reaches of the division and fortunes would deteriorate initially, the Owls slipping back into the relegation places with just seven games to play. The sale of starlet George Drury, effectively forced by the board of directors, meant McMullan had a rocky start to his Hillsborough career. But the Scot did inspire a revival, helped by the capture of internationals Bill Fallon and Charlie Napier, and four wins from those aforementioned final games ensured the trapdoor to a second consecutive relegation was avoided.

Considering the disappointment, disharmony and frustration of the previous three seasons, it was a pleasant surprise to all concerned when fortunes revived significantly in what proved to be the final pre-war season, with Wednesday challenging for promotion until the final day of the campaign. The signing of David Russell and winger Idris Lewis was seen as a positive move and, with the burgeoning talent of Jackie Robinson now beginning to flourish, Wednesday looked set for a better season. A pre-season win over Sheffield United, during a series of games held countrywide to celebrate the fiftieth birthday of the Football League, provided early impetus and Wednesday duly won four of their opening five League games to sit top of the early League table. A mini-slump followed, but a revival started in mid-November when centre-forward Doug Hunt entered the record books after scoring six times in the 7-0 home win over Norwich City. A week later, he scored a mere hat-trick during a 5-1 win at Luton Town. A run of eight wins in nine League games pushed Wednesday into the divisional top three as winter started to release its icy grip.

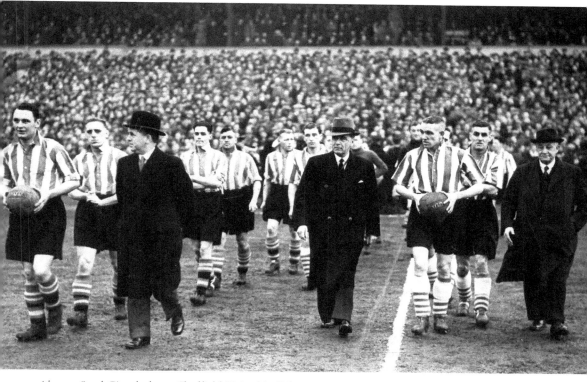

Above: Steel City derby at Sheffield United in February 1938.

Below: The 1943 War Cup final *v*. Blackpool.

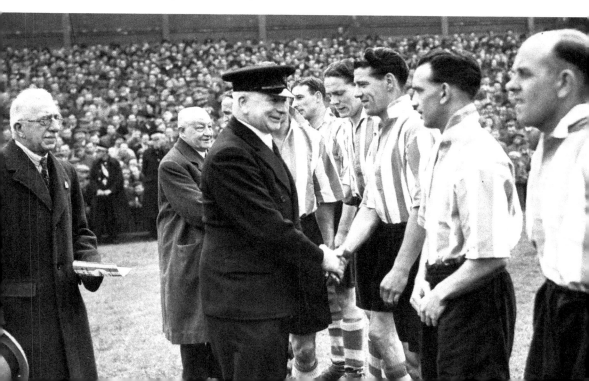

The new year saw Wednesday embark on a eight-game run in the FA Cup that commenced with a third-round replay win at non-League Yeovil Town (on the famous old sloping pitch at the Huish) and then a three-game tie with Chester, which was resolved in a second replay at Manchester City's Maine Road ground. This set up a last sixteen clash with Chelsea, which again went to a third game after a 0-0 draw at Stamford Bridge and 1-1 tie in the Hillsborough replay (over 160,000 fans watching the three matches). The so-called neutral venue of Highbury saw Chelsea progress 3-1 and left Wednesday to concentrate on a League campaign that was developing into a three-way battle for the two promotion places, with Blackburn Rovers and Sheffield United the other two contenders. Victory on the final Saturday of the season – 1-0 over Tottenham Hotspur – left Wednesday in the coveted second place, behind confirmed champions Blackburn, but unfortunately this did not mean promotion as the Blades still had one solitary game to play. A week later, a contingent of Wednesday fans were at Bramall Lane to see if Tottenham Hotspur could deny the home side and therefore seal promotion for the Owls. Unfortunately, it was not to be. United cruised to a 6-1 win, securing the second berth and leaving Wednesday agonisingly close to glory.

As the clouds of war drifted over Europe, Wednesday started the 1939/40 season with a loss at Luton Town, but only a few days later, just twenty-four hours after the Owls lost 1-0 at home to Plymouth Argyle, Britain was placed in a state of war with Germany, and all sporting activities ceased. After a few weeks of inactivity, the vast majority of clubs decided to carry on, albeit at a much reduced level: ground capacities were restricted, players were able to play on an ad hoc basis and all contracts were scrapped. The Owls were placed in the East Midlands Regional League, and just over 6,000 fans were in attendance to see four goals shared with Doncaster Rovers in the first game. Crowds were at reasonable levels in that first season, but when Sheffield became subject to heavy bombing raids in 1940, numbers plummeted, with several games being attended by less than 2,000 fans. The Christmas Day 1940 derby game between United and Wednesday was actually a Blades home fixture, but was moved to Hillsborough after Bramall Lane was badly bomb damaged. At the time it was not unusual to see teams packed with guest players, although Wednesday could usually call upon pre-war players or local amateurs to fill their team sheet on a Saturday afternoon. Two former players also made 'guest' appearances, with Wednesday borrowing back George Drury and Ronnie Starling from Arsenal and Aston Villa respectively. After that first transitional season, Wednesday subsequently played in the North Regional League and then the Football League (North). The Owls never came near to any wartime honours until the 1942/43 campaign, when the incredible goalscoring exploits of Jackie Robinson pushed them close to success. Wednesday had overcome financial problems in the early part of the war, but Robinson's astonishing record of thirty-five goals in thirty-two games took the Owls close to success in the League and led to bumper crowds, as he also helped the club reached the two-legged final of the prestigious North War Cup. One of six hat-tricks bagged by Robinson came in an 8-2 win over Sheffield United, and he scored a brace as the Blades were beaten over two legs to reach the last four of the knock-out cup (the two games were watched by over 80,000 fans). A 4-1 aggregate win over York City clinched a meeting with Blackpool in the final, but after a 2-2 draw in Lancashire, the Owls lost 2-1 at home in front of the biggest wartime crowd at Hillsborough (crowd restrictions having been removed some time earlier). As the war started to turn the way of the Allies, football slowly returned to normal, with the FA Cup reintroduced

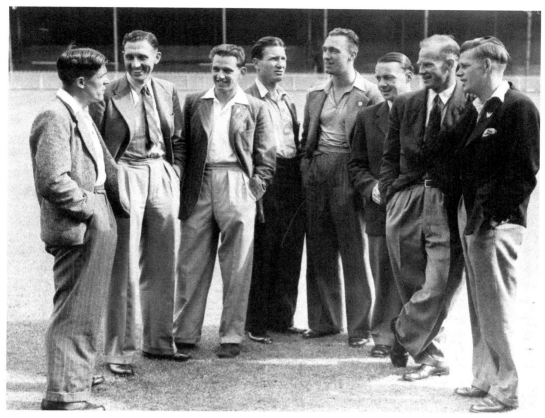

Above: Players having a natter, July 1946.

Below: Match action, Wednesday *v.* Newcastle, May 1947.

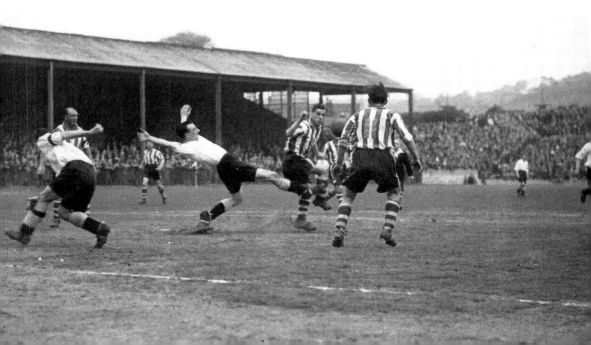

in the 1945/46 season – all games uniquely played over two legs until the semi-final stage – and national League football restarted a year later. The Owls reached the last sixteen of the FA Cup in 1946 (the reserve team also winning the reformed Central League), and returned to their nineteenth-century roots by sporting a natty blue-and-white hooped kit on a matchday.

POST-WAR CROWD BOOM

When League football returned in 1946, the fixtures from the abandoned 1939/40 season were simply repeated, but the effects of the conflict on playing personnel were obvious. Of the eleven men who played in the opening-day 4-1 loss at Luton Town, only Jackie Robinson had appeared in the same game seven years earlier. The man now in charge was Eric Taylor, having taken over from Jimmy McMullan in 1942, and it must have quickly become obvious to him that Wednesday were not really prepared for the return of the 'beautiful game'. In fact, it would be an almost season-long fight against relegation into the regional leagues for Wednesday – Division Three was split into North and South sections in those days. The Owls recorded only a dozen wins all season, in a campaign that was badly affected by one of the worst winters on record. A highlight was a 5-1 Hillsborough win over Tottenham Hotspur, new centre-forward Jimmy Dailey netting a hat-trick. Thankfully, Wednesday did manage to stave off relegation to finish in twentieth place, just three points above Swansea Town, who went down with Welsh neighbours Newport County. The final day of the season was notable as Wednesday finished their fixtures on the first Saturday in June, easily the latest finish to any season, and Chesterfield player George Milburn achieved the rare feat of scoring a hat-trick of penalties in the Owls' 4-2 loss at Saltergate. The first post-war season saw the Owls finish in what, at the time, was their worst-ever League position. The club publicly stated that this was not good enough and strenuous efforts would be made to improve the situation. A decade after a failure to invest cost the club their First Division place, the late 1940s proved the complete opposite, the Owls' board sanctioning a series of record-breaking acquisitions. The club transfer record was first broken in 1947 when a fee of £12,000 brought Eddie Quigley from Bury, and with the new man in the attack, the Owls overcame a mixed start to steadily climb the table. A run of six consecutive wins in just seventeen days took the side into a promotion-challenging position, but a crucial loss to eventual runners-up Newcastle United contributed to a final finishing position of fourth, five points behind the promoted Geordies. New man Quigley proved to be money well spent as he notched twenty-three goals in just thirty-two appearances, and hopes were high that promotion would be secured in the following campaign. The club's record transfer mark tumbled again early in the 1948/49 season as a £20,000 fee (equalling the British record) brought winger Eddie Kilshaw to Hillsborough. Unfortunately for both parties concerned, Kilshaw's career would come to a premature end through injury, after just nineteen games in the blue-and-white stripes. He joined a side that were sitting comfortably in the League top ten, but which had failed to really mount a serious challenge for the top two positions. Inconsistent form meant the Owls were rarely in the top six, and after climbing to eighth place in early April, they remained there until the end of the season, disappointingly finishing quite a distance off the business end of

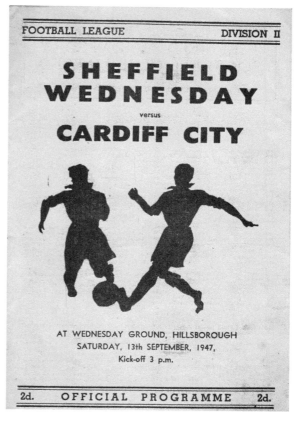

Right: Classic programme cover from 1947.

Below: Ticket from Owls *v.* Blades on the Isle of Man.

I. O. M. F. A.	ISLE OF MAN FOOTBALL ASSOCIATION. 2887
2887 Football Match SHEFFIELD U. v SHEFFIELD W. Whit-Monday, 17th May, 1948. KICK-OFF 3-30. GROUND TICKET 2/6 THIS PORTION TO BE RETAINED.	GRAND FOOTBALL MATCH (By Special Permission of English Football Association.) SHEFFIELD UNITED VERSUS SHEFFIELD WEDNESDAY King George V Park, Belle Vue, Douglas, I.o.M. WHIT-MONDAY, MAY 17TH 1948. KICK-OFF 3-30 P.M. ADMIT TO GROUND. TICKET .. ... 2/6 Proceeds for Insular Football. V.P. Ltd. THIS PORTION TO BE GIVEN UP.

the Second Division table. Despite Wednesday failing to gain promotion, the club, like the vast majority in the British game, was experiencing a huge boom in crowds as a public starved of football in the war years flocked back to English League grounds. The first season after the war saw the Owls average just under 27,000 through the Hillsborough gates, but by the end of the 1940s, this figure had risen to over 40,000, handing Wednesday a welcome boost to the coffers.

PROMOTION AT LAST, FOLLOWED BY THE YO-YO YEARS

The promotion promise was finally delivered in 1950, after the Owls made an excellent start to the season and quickly moved into second position in the table. Eddie Quigley and Clarrie Jordan grabbed individual four-goal hauls against Chesterfield and Hull City respectively, while winger Charlie Tomlinson scored after just twelve seconds at Preston North End – the quickest recorded goal in Owls history. The sale of star attacker Eddie Quigley for a British record £26,000 fee looked a strange decision, and failure to win any of the opening eight games of 1950, including a FA Cup exit against top-flight Arsenal, looked to have dashed hopes of promotion – Wednesday slipping down to fifth place. Thankfully, though, they recovered and back-to-back wins over Easter put the club back into the coveted second promotion spot. A treble from new signing Walter Rickett in the penultimate home game helped beat Grimsby Town 4-1 and moved Wednesday to the brink, but the promotion issue would go down to the wire, with a nervous 50,000-plus crowd packed into Hillsborough on the final day to see the outcome. In a reverse of the finish to the 1938/39 season, Sheffield United had this time finished their fixtures and, along with fellow promotion rivals Southampton, could only hope that the result at Hillsborough would work to their advantage. The vagaries of the old goal average system (goals scored divided by goals conceded) meant the possibilities were endless, but Wednesday knew that a win or a 0-0 draw would secure a First Division place. A fraught afternoon ensued as Wednesday and champions Tottenham Hotspur failed to conjure a goal, and home fans could celebrate the end of a thirteen-year exile from the top echelon of the domestic game.

Whereas goal average helped the Owls to promotion in 1950, a year later it proved their downfall as a long and disappointing season ended with a last-day relegation, despite thrashing Everton in the final game of the campaign. The season opened with a heavy defeat at Chelsea, but a thrilling win over reigning champions Portsmouth would prove only a minor highlight as the Owls quickly slipped to the wrong end of the table and never really recovered. Despite the club's precarious position, they did not lack ambition and on 15 March 1951, the Owls smashed the British transfer record when they paid Notts County £35,000 for star forward Jackie Sewell. The signing was seen by many as a last-ditch attempt to avoid the drop, and the new man duly netted on his debut and scored a further five goals before the season's close. A run of three consecutive wins in April 1951 raised hopes and briefly took Wednesday out of the bottom two, before a loss at Tottenham Hotspur dumped them right back in trouble. It was again left to the final day of the season, and the Owls knew that nothing less than a 6-0 win would give them

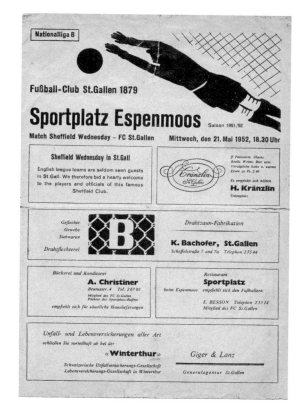

Left: Tour programme from Switzerland in 1952.

Below: Poignant image of Derek Dooley post injury.

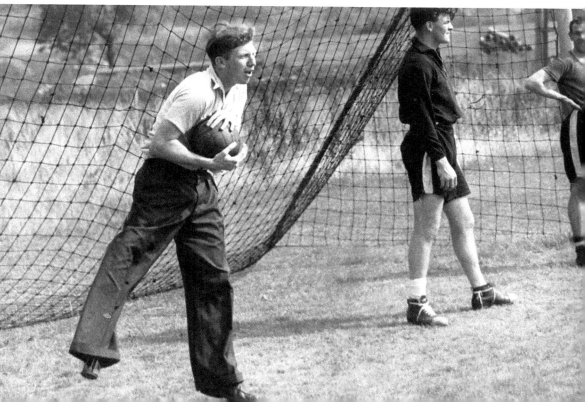

any chance. Incredibly, watched by 41,166, Everton were beaten by that margin. But the score proved academic as rivals Chelsea won 4-0, sending Wednesday and their Liverpool opponents down into the Second Division. Hopes were high of a quick return to the First Division, but by mid-October the side were languishing in the bottom half of the table after suffering three consecutive defeats. Then a decision by manager Eric Taylor changed the course of Wednesday history, and launched the career of a battering-ram-style centre-forward. A young Derek Dooley had only briefly featured at senior level for the Owls, making his debut against Preston North End in October 1949, but a flurry of reserve team goals early in the 1951/52 season convinced Wednesday that he was worth another run in the side. The rest, as they say, is history. Dooley bagged a brace against Barnsley in what was only his third game for the Owls, and then embarked on a quite remarkable goalscoring run. A few weeks later, Dooley scored five second-half goals against Notts County, and he ended the season with an astonishing forty-six goals in only thirty League games – a record that will surely stand for all time as the biggest-ever seasonal haul by a Wednesday player. Other records tumbled as well – he scored in nine consecutive games at the latter end of 1951 – while crowds flocked to see the scoring phenomenon. A new record crowd for a Hillsborough League fixture – 65,384 – attended the Steel City derby in January 1952. Unsurprisingly, his goals powered a rejuvenated Owls side up the League table, and it was fitting that a Dooley brace beat Coventry City in the final away game and clinched promotion back to the top flight. He then netted in the last day 2-2 home draw with West Ham United (Wednesday's 100th goal in the League) to secure the championship. Fans could not wait until the next season so their new goal machine could be unleashed on the top division!

Sadly, the 1952/53 season will be remembered mainly for the events on one specific day – 14 February 1953. Wednesday travelled to Preston North End on that Saturday and were comfortably sitting in mid-table, overcoming a poor start to the season to climb the standings in the winter months. Star man Dooley had adapted well to life in the top tier, boasting sixteen League goals in twenty-eight games. That fateful day started with sad news, club chairman William Fearehough had passed away, breaking a family link that stretched all the back to the very formation of the club. The Owls subsequently lost the game at Deepdale 1-0 and were rocked when a collision between Dooley and the North End 'keeper led to the former suffering a broken right leg and being taken to Preston Royal Infirmary. Fans were obviously disappointed that their big No. 9 would miss the rest of the season, but this turned to shock and disbelief a mere forty-eight hours later when the hospital announced that due to an infection, probably contracted while he lay prone on the playing surface, gas gangrene had taken hold and they had no option but to save his life by amputating his right leg. The news rocked the whole football world. Dooley's meteoric rise to national prominence had ended, and one of the most popular players in Owls' history faced an uncertain future. The remainder of the season was played out in a somewhat gloomy atmosphere, with a few men failing to fill Dooley's considerable boots.

After the sad end to Dooley's career, crowds at Hillsborough dropped 15 per cent on the previous season (a club record 42,539 average), despite the Owls finishing in a reasonably comfortable nineteenth place after a poor end to the campaign. The return to Deepdale ended in a 6-0 thrashing, but an FA Cup run to the last four was a real highlight; Sheffield United (3-1 in a Bramall Lane replay), Chesterfield (also in a replay), Everton and Bolton Wanderers were beaten to set up a Maine Road semi-final. A crowd of over 75,000 were inside the Manchester ground, but it was 'bogey team' Preston North End who ended dreams of Wembley, winning

Dated 1st October, 19 56.

THE

Sheffield Wednesday

Football Club

AND

JOHN FANTHAM.

38, Annesley Road,

Sheffield, 8.

AGREEMENT

FOR HIRE OF A PLAYER

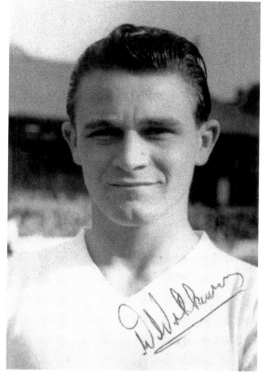

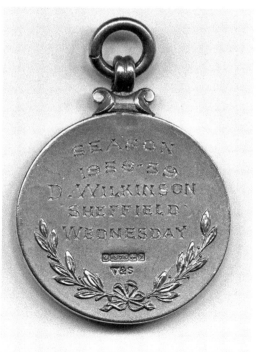

Above left: Contract of post-war record scorer John Fantham.

Above right: Winger Derek Wilkinson (1954–64).

Right: Second Division Championship medal.

2-0 on the day. Seasonal top scorer was winger Dennis Woodhead, with twenty-one League and Cup goals, and Dooley's old shirt was worn by the likes of Jack Shaw and John Jordan, both of whom contributed reasonable goal tallies in what was a transitional season. Unfortunately, the club struggled to overcome the loss of their ginger-haired talisman and suffered a disastrous 1954/55 season, which ended with Wednesday occupying the wooden spoon position in the First Division. Crowds again fell away dramatically – the average at Hillsborough having fallen by almost 40 per cent from Dooley's heyday – although the club's poor form could certainly be argued as a contributory factor. The season started with back-to-back 4-2 defeats to Wolves and Manchester United. A 6-3 home win over Aston Villa proved a false dawn as by early November the Owls had slipped to twenty-second position and remained on the bottom rung for the remainder of the campaign. Wednesday also laboured over beating non-League Hastings United in the FA Cup, while arguably the highlight of the whole season came in March 1955, when Hillsborough hosted Derek Dooley's benefit game. A crowd of 55,000 attended a Sheffield XI versus International XI game, which also doubled up as the first match to be played officially under floodlights at the ground – the system having been installed the previous summer. The international side won 5-1, with the considerable receipts ensuring that Dooley's benefit fund increased significantly, allowing the stricken forward to forget any short-term financial worries.

The summer of 1955 was again a time to restructure, with Dr Andrew Stephen appointed chairman and secretary-manager Taylor adding several new faces to his squad in an attempt to bounce back. New men included Isle of Wight-born centre-forward Roy Shiner, winger Albert Broadbent and defensive players Ron Staniforth and Walter Bingley. It was, however, record signing Jackie Sewell who grabbed an opening-day treble as the Owls got off to a flying start, beating Plymouth Argyle 5-2 at Hillsborough, before a 3-0 win at Liverpool took them top of the early League table. A plethora of draws meant a fall back down the table, but a 4-0 Christmas Eve win over Stoke City saw the Owls reclaim top spot, and it was a position they did not relinquish. The home game with Barnsley in March 1956 became the first League game to be played under lights at Hillsborough, while a 5-2 win at Bury, in the final away game of the campaign, not only clinched promotion but also the championship shield for the second time in four years. New signing Shiner proved a big favourite with Owls fans, being ever present and contributing thirty-three goals in an Owls total of 101 in the League. It was therefore back to the First Division for the 1956/57 season, and Wednesday made a great start, winning four of their opening seven League fixtures to sit just outside the top six. A treble from winger Alan Finney in a 4-1 home win over Spurs stopped a run of five consecutive defeats, but the Owls remained in the bottom half of the table for the rest of the season, a late flurry of wins taking them up to a satisfactory fourteenth-place finish. Despite playing three games in the FA Cup, Wednesday failed to get past the third round, losing in a second replay at Goodison Park against Preston North End, while England international inside-forward Albert Quixall finished top of the club's scoring charts with twenty-two League goals to his name.

With secretary-manager Eric Taylor handed a new five-year contract and the club's youngsters reaching the FA Youth Cup semi-final for the first time (losing over two legs to West Ham United). hopes were high that Wednesday could push on after consolidating. Unfortunately, a delayed start to the 1957/58 season – after a flu bug caused the two opening games to be postponed – meant the Owls got off to a sluggish start and quickly slipped to the wrong end of the League table. Home wins over Leeds United and Arsenal briefly lifted the club off the bottom of the table, but defeats to Preston North End and Nottingham Forest ensured they ended the calendar year back at the bottom. League worries were briefly put aside in the New Year when a win at non-League Hereford United and a home success over Hull City set up a fifth-round tie at Manchester United. However, by the time the match was eventually played, only the most die-hard Owls fans actually wanted their side to win, it being the home side's first game since the Munich Air Disaster, which had decimated the Red Devils' playing ranks. The match programme poignantly left the Manchester United team blank and, on a sea of emotion, Wednesday could offer no resistance, losing 3-0 on the night in front of almost 60,000 at Old Trafford. It was back to the perilous position in the League standings, and though Wednesday did briefly drag themselves out of the bottom two places, it proved a mere blip as the Owls suffered relegation for the third time in the decade – a 5-0 home win on the final day of the season proving merely academic.

Despite the trials and tribulations of the 1957/58 season, there were some positives to emerge, with the signing of future England international custodian Ron Springett. The Owls had tried a total of four different 'keepers prior to the arrival of the new man from Queens Park Rangers, while the emergence of John Fantham and Tony Kay bode well for the club's future. The summer of 1958 saw a significant change in the managerial structure at the club. The old role of secretary-manager, held by Eric Taylor, was effectively split into two, with Taylor concentrating on the administration side of the club's operations and Wednesday advertising for their first-ever 'football manager'. They did initially approach Tottenham Hotspur boss Bill Nicholson – who would lead Spurs to the famous double in 1961 – but when he turned down the opportunity they instead turned to a relative unknown, Rochdale boss Harry Catterick. The appointment of the Darlington-born former Everton player would, however, prove an inspired choice by the Owls. His new charges made a blistering start to the 1958/59 campaign, winning eleven of the opening thirteen games of the season, and scoring forty-one goals. The period also saw the big money move of 'golden boy' Albert Quixall – for a British record £45,000 transfer fee – to Manchester United, as Matt Busby started to rebuild his decimated squad. The September game at Sunderland also saw history made, as Derek and Eric Wilkinson became the first and only twins to ever appear in a competitive senior game for the Owls. Despite a 2-0 FA Cup home defeat to Newcastle United, watched by over 50,000 fans, Wednesday's form in the League continued to be remarkably consistent, with wins and goals flowing unabated. A home win over Liverpool – with still four games left to play – secured the fourth promotion that decade, and a 5-0 home success over neighbours Barnsley (watched bizarrely by the lowest crowd of the season) duly clinched yet another Second Division championship shield. The goals (106) and points (62) were both club records, and Wednesday returned to the top flight in emphatic fashion. Roy Shiner again topped the goalscoring chart, netting twenty-eight in thirty-eight League appearances.

RISE & FALL...

The constant promotion and relegation cycle of the 1950s finally came to an end in the final season of the decade when Wednesday made a big impression on their return to the top division, finishing the season in the club's highest position (fifth) since the mid-1930s. A goal from John

Fantham secured an excellent opening-day win at Arsenal – the Sheffield born inside-forward would end the season as top scorer with eighteen League and Cup goals – and although the club's early-season form was inconsistent, the Owls started to slowly climb the table, while also enjoying a run to the semi-final of the FA Cup. Revival in the League started with a remarkable run just before the Christmas period, when the Owls won four out of five games – including 7-0 and 5-1 home wins over West Ham United and Arsenal respectively – and scored a total of twenty-one goals. That rapid accrual of points pushed Wednesday into the divisional top six by early January 1960, and that great form was carried into the FA Cup, where huge crowds watched the Owls' progress in the competition. Over 100,000 fans attended home wins over Middlesbrough and non-League Peterborough United before 66,350 watched a Tom McAnearney penalty secure a 1-0 replay win at Manchester United. This set up a Steel City derby at Bramall Lane in the quarter-final, and Wednesday earned both the 'bragging rights' and a place in the last four after a Derek Wilkinson double took the Owls through. This meant a Maine Road clash with Blackburn Rovers for a trip to Wembley. Despite a second-half strike from John Fantham, the Owls could not force a replay, and in front of almost 75,000 it was the Lancashire club who progressed. The season finished with Wednesday just six points behind champions Burnley. Catterick had assembled a side that could again challenge for the major domestic prizes, and fans genuinely hoped that the yo-yo years were well and truly in the past. Just after the 1959/60 season came to a close, the Owls embarked on an ambitious tour of the former Soviet Union, playing twice in Moscow and once in Tbilisi – now in modern-day Georgia – although the huge mileage covered made it a tiring end-of-season tour for the leg-weary players.

Manager Catterick was clearly happy with his playing personnel, as no significant transfer activity took place in the summer of 1960, and his opinion was proved correct when Wednesday emerged as the major rival to Tottenham Hotspur for the championship crown. The Owls were beaten only once in the opening sixteen games of the season, which included a titanic meeting with a Spurs side who arrived at Hillsborough still unbeaten and with a sizeable lead at the top of the division. It was a game that the Owls simply had to win and it probably left the Wednesday hierarchy cursing their decision to knock down the old North Stand the previous summer and begin construction on a state-of-the-art 10,000-seater cantilever structure. This meant that Hillsborough was a three-sided ground for the whole of the 1960/61 season and, in hindsight, a new ground record for a League game would surely have been set at the Spurs match – 56,363 crammed into the three sides available on the day. Those that did attend witnessed a thrilling game as goals from Billy Griffin and John Fantham helped their side to a 2-1 success and put a temporary halt on their opponents' seemingly unstoppable march at the summit of the League.

Straight after the win over Spurs, the Owls suffered three consecutive League losses to dampen hopes of catching the Londoners, while a 5-1 half-time lead against Blackburn Rovers was almost surrendered as Wednesday hung on to win by the odd goal in nine. As in the previous season, Wednesday also went on an incredible run of games where they piled up goals and victories, recording five League wins in a row, including a 6-1 win at Fulham (the home side scoring in the wrong net from the kick-off without a Wednesday play touching the ball) and a 5-1 home success over Preston North End. During that run of games they also recorded one of the best results in their entire history as the Owls went goal crazy to thrash Manchester United 7-2 (Keith Ellis 3, Fantham 2, Alan Finney 2) in a FA Cup fourth round replay at Old Trafford and progress into the fifth round of the tournament. The Cup run ended at Burnley in a sixth-round replay. The race for the title came to a conclusion at White Hart Lane in April 1961, when Spurs beat the Owls 2-1 to clinch the League – Wednesday eventually finishing eight points behind their London rivals in the runners-up spot.

Despite the Owls finishing in their highest position since the war, all was not well behind the scenes. Relations between highly rated boss Harry Catterick and the Wednesday board became strained in early spring when the club failed to sanction a big money move for centre-forward Joe Baker. It was the first time in Catterick's tenure that he had asked the club to loosen the purse strings, as he believed the signing would lead to Wednesday winning the League title in 1961/62. The failure of the board to give the green light to the transfer would have long-term ramifications. In early April 1961, Catterick tendered his resignation and moved to his boyhood club Everton soon after, where he would lead the Toffeemen to the League championship. He left with four games remaining, secretary Eric Taylor taking charge for the rest of the campaign, and it would be fair to say that the Owls would not realistically challenge for the title again until the outstanding team of the early 1990s. The season will also be remembered for a distressing incident on Boxing Day 1960, when the Owls team coach crashed on an icy road near Huntingdon on the way back from a game at Arsenal. Several players received cuts and bruises, but young professional Dougie McMillan was trapped in the wreckage and the attending emergency services had no other option than to amputate the Scot's right leg – the similarities with Derek Dooley, almost eight years earlier, being sadly obvious.

The Owls were invited into the Fairs Cup – a forerunner of the modern-day Europa League – by the organising committee in the summer of 1961, but they first had to appoint a manager to lead the club's first assault on Europe. The new man at the helm proved to be forward-thinking ex-Ajax Amsterdam boss Vic Buckingham, who had actually agreed to return from Holland to take over at Plymouth Argyle before a change of heart brought him north. Buckingham – who is generally credited with 'discovering' Dutch legend Johan Cryuff – was somewhat of a laid-back character who liked his players to express themselves on the pitch, and Owls fans waited to see if the side could follow on from the fine form of the previous season. The old adage of 'if it ain't broke don't fix it' certainly applied in the close season as the new manager made no signings of note, relying on the same squad that had impressed so greatly in the two seasons since the Owls regained their First Division place. The new manager could not have hoped for a better start. The Owls won their opening three games of the new season and netted eleven goals in the process. The 4-2 home success over Bolton Wanderers also saw the club officially open the impressive new all-seated £150,000 North Stand with FIFA President Sir Stanley Rous cutting the proverbial ribbon. The club's first-ever game in European football was played on French soil, and Lyon recorded a 4-2 win before the Owls progressed on aggregate; winning 5-2 in the return leg in front of just over 30,000 fans. A hat-trick from Gerry Young helped to see off AS Roma 4-0 at Hillsborough in the next round – a 1-0 second-leg loss in Italy proving academic – to set up a glamour tie with Spanish giants Barcelona at the quarter-final stage. In the intervening weeks, Wednesday's League form was fairly consistent, with a position in the top half of the division maintained without really threatening the top spot. A run in the FA Cup ended at the last sixteen stage – over 130,000 watching two meetings as Manchester United won in a Hillsborough replay – while a bout of icy weather looked set to force the postponement of the first-leg home tie against Barcelona. Thankfully, the game did go ahead on the scheduled date, the inclement conditions being a major factor in an attendance of less than 29,000, and the Owls secured a 3-2

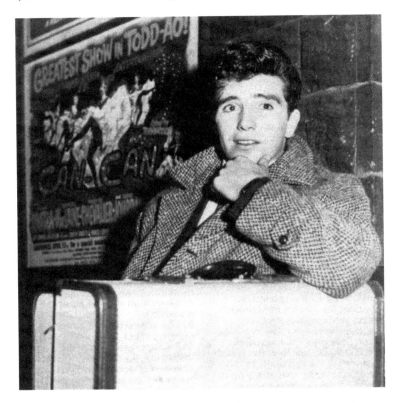

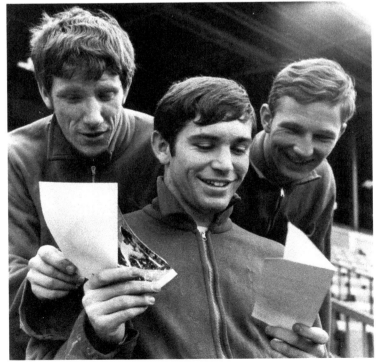

Below left: Ian Branfoot, Sam Ellis and Jack Whitham *c.* 1965.

Above left: John Quinn at Sheffield Station prior to USSR tour (1960).

Opposite above: Manager Harry Catterick and secretary Eric Taylor *c.* 1961.

Opposite below: Wednesday *v.* Preston North End, February 1961.

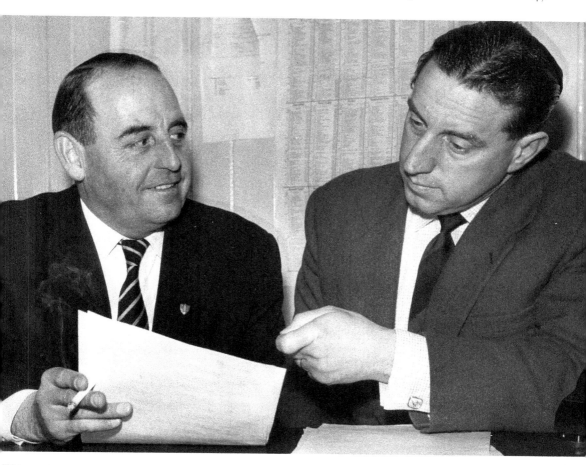

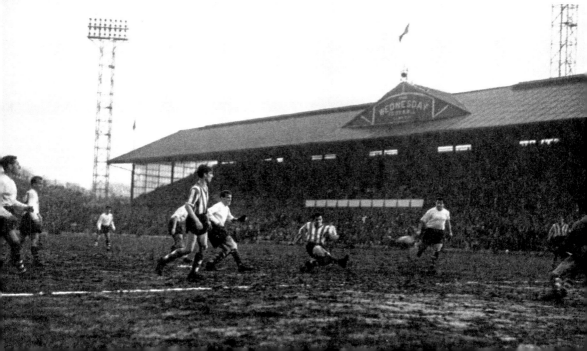

win to leave the tie in the balance prior to the trip to Spain. A crowd of 75,000 were inside the Nou Camp for the return where, despite a valiant effort from Wednesday, the Catalan side won 2-0 to secure a place in the semi-finals.

Back in the League, a late run of wins lifted the Owls into a respectable sixth place. However, the club's newly installed manager was not altogether happy with his charges. In March 1962, he was front-page news in the local paper as he sensationally slated his own players, citing a lack of skill on their part. It has never been reported what the players thought of his outburst and it was soon forgotten, as the summer of 1962 was dominated by an almighty row between the organisers of the Fairs Cup and the English authorities, which directly affected the Owls. Wednesday, who also captured the signature of highly rated centre-forward David 'Bronco' Layne from Bradford City in the close season, had been invited by the organising committee of the competition, along with two other English sides. However, the Football Association and Football League then decided to nominate their own choice of three clubs and effectively banned any other side from competing. The row rumbled on all the way through the summer – Wednesday were even included in the first-round draw – but the intransigent attitude of the English authorities eventually left them acutely embarrassed as an understandably frustrated Fairs Cup committee reduced their invitation to a single English club with Wednesday not in possession of the 'golden ticket'.

The disappointment of missing out on European football overshadowed the start of the new season. The 1962/63 campaign would be dominated by the horrendous winter, with the Owls failing to play a single League fixture for almost two months early in 1963. Before the big freeze, secretary Eric Taylor had pulled the proverbial 'rabbit out of the hat' by securing the visit of famous Brazilian club Santos to Hillsborough, along with their incomparable No. 10, Pelé. An incredible crowd of over 45,000 ensured that Wednesday made a profit from the visit, while Owls supporters, and local football fans in general, had the rare opportunity to see the legendary player in the flesh – for many years supporters still talked about the penalty scored by Pelé, which saw Ron Springett rooted to the spot as the ball flew past him. The visit of Santos effectively spelt the end of high-profile exhibition games at Hillsborough, which had started in the mid-1950s when floodlights were installed, although the huge crowd did suggest that an appetite remained among the footballing public of the city. Off the field news saw Hillsborough awarded several games in the 1966 World Cup finals – another honour attributed to master administrator Eric Taylor. Wednesday again finished in sixth position in the First Division, despite suffering a poor run of form that saw them fail to win any of the final ten League games of the 1962 calendar year. The club's FA Cup third-round tie at Shrewsbury Town, scheduled for early January 1963, took over two months to complete as huge falls of snow paralysed large parts of the country. Wednesday, now sporting a new thin-striped shirt, exited the Cup at Arsenal in the next round, but a late run of five straight League wins, including a 3-1 derby success over the Blades, pushed them to another respectable finish. New signing Layne proved a huge success in the top division, scoring a terrific twenty-nine League goals in thirty-nine appearances to more than reward the Owls for the sizeable fee paid to bring the attacker to Hillsborough.

After the controversy of the previous summer, the English authorities did not intervene when the Fairs Cup committee sent an invitation to the Owls in the close season of 1963. Wednesday were duly drawn against Dutch club DOS Utrecht, while the new season started with a thrilling 3-3 home game against Manchester United. However, it would prove a poor start for

Buckingham's men as Wednesday struggled badly and found themselves down in seventeenth place when they travelled across the water for their opening Fairs Cup engagement. The subsequent 4-1 win in Holland, followed by the same score in the second leg, boosted confidence somewhat, and by the Christmas programme, the Owls had climbed into the top four. The run in Europe ended against German side Cologne, the Owls exiting 4-3 on aggregate. January 1964 saw Wednesday victims of a Cup upset when minnows Newport County won 3-2 in South Wales, leaving Wednesday to 'concentrate on the League'. A third consecutive sixth-place finish was secured, but unfortunately the whole season was overshadowed by the events of April 1964, when manager Vic Buckingham resigned from his post and football was rocked by the infamous bribes scandal, which pointed a finger at several people, including key Wednesday players. The departure of Buckingham seemed almost inevitable – he had fallen out with England 'keeper Ron Springett, who'd asked for a transfer, and had a supposedly rocky relationship with his chief scout, Jack Mansell. His assistant, Gordon Clark, then left to take over at Peterborough, and the Owls board duly informed Buckingham that his contract would not be renewed. Unsurprisingly, he decided not to remain in the post and left immediately, with Eric Taylor handed the caretaker role to take Wednesday through to the end of the season.

However, the departure of the Owls' boss paled in significance to the events of 12 April 1964, when the *Sunday People* newspaper broke a story that several professional players had placed bets on their own side to lose. Sadly for the Owls, two of the men involved were vital members of their side: captain and England international Peter Swan, and prolific centre-forward David Layne. The two men involved were immediately suspended (a third ex-Owl involved was Tony Kay, who had moved to Everton) and a clearly distressed Eric Taylor gave an impassioned speech before the home game with Spurs, which was played the day after the story broke. The monies involved seem almost trivial, but unfortunately the story shook the public's confidence in the game and the FA duly banned all the players involved *sine die*, effectively imposing a lifetime ban. All involved subsequently served prison sentences and, in hindsight, the loss of such key players was a blow that Wednesday never really recovered from. It would not be until the mid-1980s that the Owls again posted a top-six finish in the First Division. After the dust had settled on the events of April 1964, the Owls' first task was to appoint a new manager, and their choice was a surprise. Alan Brown had just taken Sunderland to promotion from the second tier, but he duly left the North East club to sign a five-year contract at Hillsborough. In comparison with his predecessor, Brown was much more of a disciplinarian, although his somewhat harsh persona did mask a warm personality that would help the club greatly as youth came to the fore in the few seasons that followed. Wednesday started the 1964/65 season on tour in Germany, facing Werder Bremen and Kaiserslautern, and throughout the remainder of the 1960s the club became the atypical globetrotters as pre- and post-season foreign trips encompassed visits to Bulgaria, Singapore, Hong Kong, Malaysia, Denmark, Spain, Poland, Mexico, Holland, Austria, France and Italy!

Brown's first season in charge started with a 1-0 home success over Blackburn Rovers, and the new manager would have been pleased to see Wednesday enjoy a steady season, which resulted in a final position of eighth, just two points shy of the top six. The season saw several young players introduced into the side, including Howard Wilkinson, Brian Usher and Wilf Smith, while the restructuring of the team continued in 1965/66 as several of the 'old guard' departed, including the unfortunate Mark Pearson and Derek Wilkinson, both of whom never played for

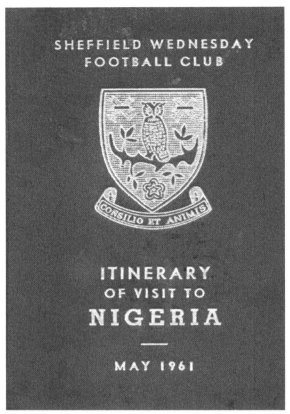

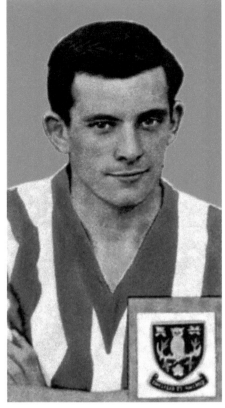

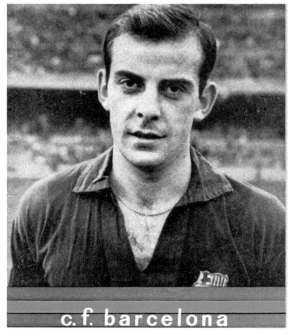

Above left: Club itinerary for the 1961 tour of Nigeria.

Above right: John Fantham (1958–69), 166 goals in 434 games.

Left: Programme for Fairs Cup tie at the Nou Camp, March 1962.

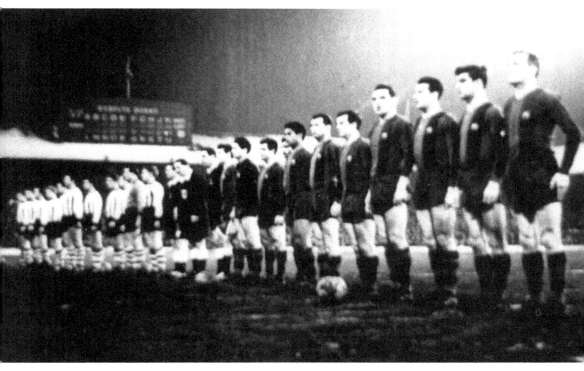

Above: The teams – Wednesday *v.* Barcelona, February 1962.

Below: The players at Scarborough, 1963.

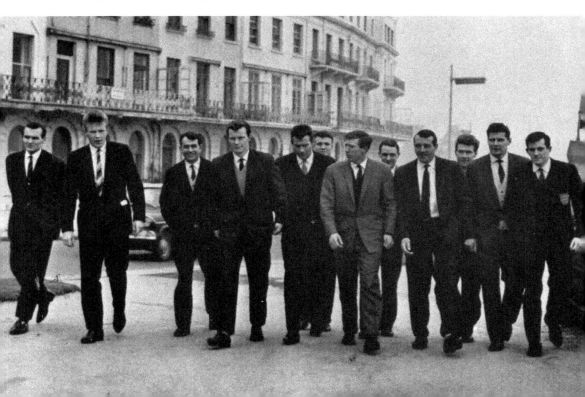

the Owls again after suffering serious injuries. One huge change in the summer of 1965 was a controversial move from the traditional blue-and-white striped home shirt to one with a full blue body and white arms – the radical decision going down like a lead balloon with the vast majority of Wednesday fans! The Owls League form in the new campaign was patchy, but all that was forgotten in the New Year as a young side went all the way to Wembley in the FA Cup, becoming the first team to achieve the feat without playing a single tie at home. A few months earlier, highly promising young attacker David Ford had made history as the club's first used substitute and, along with teenager Jim McCalliog (bought from Chelsea for a sizeable fee), he was pivotal in the Cup run. The run started with a 3-2 win at Reading, and Wednesday reached the last sixteen after winning 2-1 against a Newcastle United side that had beaten them in the League just a week earlier. Almost 50,000 packed into Huddersfield Town's old Leeds Road ground to see the Owls go through to the quarter-finals on an awful mud bath of a pitch – David Ford and Brian Usher with the goals in another 2-1 victory. A brace from Ford then led Wednesday to the now common 2-1 success, at Blackburn Rovers. On another horrendous playing surface at Villa Park for the semi-final, the Owls shocked the experts by beating hot favourites Chelsea 2-0 thanks to goals from emerging youngster Graham Pugh and a last-minute strike from former Chelsea player McCalliog. Back in the League, Wednesday struggled somewhat and the fixture pile-up caused by the FA Cup meant that they played four games in eight days at the end of the season, losing the final three to slip to a disappointing seventeenth place in the table. However, Wednesday fans had a trip to Wembley to look forward to and, in front of a 100,000-strong crowd, it seemed like the old trophy would be returning to Sheffield for the first time since pre-war days, as goals from McCalliog and Ford put the Owls two goals ahead early in the second half. Unfortunately, though, it was not to be and it was agony for fans as Everton, managed of course by former Owls boss Catterick, fought back to win 3-2 and leave Brown's young side gallant losers – captain Don Megson starting a tradition when he led his team around the pitch on a lap of honour.

The summer of 1966 was, of course, a vintage period for the national side, as England lifted the Jules Rimet Trophy at Wembley, with Hillsborough hosting several games in the tournament. On the domestic front, Wednesday, despite the Cup final loss, looked to have a bright future, with a whole host of young players having emerged, and crowds would increase significantly in the 1966/67 season, helped by the aforementioned World Cup win on home soil, with an average of 30,629 supporters attending the twenty-one home League fixtures. The Owls made a great start and remained unbeaten in their opening seven League games to sit in the divisional top two in mid-September, with neighbours Rotherham United the only team to lower their colours when a last-minute winner condemned Wednesday to defeat at Hillsborough – the club's first-ever tie in the Football League Cup. Unfortunately, form in the League quickly turned into a winless run of nine games, despite the big money signing of centre-forward John Ritchie. Wednesday slipped down to mid-table where they remained for the rest of the campaign, but a late rally saw them end in eleventh place. Highlights were 5-0 and 7-0 home wins over Sunderland and Burnley respectively, with the win against the Lancashire club notable for a treble from David Ford and two goals from substitute Jack Whitham – the first player to score for the Owls after entering the fray from the bench. The FA Cup run went to the quarter-finals this time, with the third-round home tie against Queens Park Rangers seeing Wednesday introduce a new mascot, Ozzie the Owl, to the home fans. The next round saw Mansfield Town at Hillsborough and the game was memorable for sixteen-year-old custodian Gary Scothorn, who became the youngest ever player to appear for the Owls at the time – he kept a clean sheet in a 4-0 win. The run ended when Chelsea grabbed a last-minute winner at Stamford Bridge. The summer of 1967 was notable for the unique transfer that resulted in the Springett brothers, Ron and Peter, swapping clubs, the former England international 'keeper moving back to QPR, with younger sibling Peter, also a goalkeeper, moving north to Sheffield.

The 1967/68 campaign saw season ticket prices for a South Stand seat at Hillsborough break the double-figure barrier for the first time, moving to £10 from £8 8s, which meant fans paid a rough equivalent of £140 in today's prices for a season pass. However, the rise did not dampen enthusiasm among Wednesday fans, and the club averaged 31,736 for home games – the last time the Owls averaged over the notable 30,000 mark. Victories in their first two home games, allied with an opening-day 3-2 win against a West Ham United side packed with World Cup winners such as Moore and Hurst, took the Owls to the top of the table. The home game with Fulham saw the club celebrate its centenary, and it was rather fitting that victory took the Owls back to the top of the division. Unfortunately, Wednesday failed to publicise the fact that supporters would be admitted for half price, resulting in one of the lowest crowds of the season! Great starts followed by equally big slumps were a common theme of the mid- to late 1960s, and Wednesday endured a terrible run in the second half of the season, winning only two of their final twenty-two League games to slide dramatically down the table and finish just outside the bottom two relegation places, in nineteenth spot. There was some comfort in Cup football as Wednesday reached the last sixteen of both the FA and League Cup, bowing out to old foes Chelsea in the former and Stoke City in the latter. The campaign also saw the departure of manager Alan Brown, who tendered his resignation in February 1968, a few days after his former club Sunderland dispensed with the services of their manager. He vehemently denied he was set to take over at the Wearside club, but it was no surprise when he was appointed soon after departing Hillsborough. His assistant, Jack Marshall, who himself had only joined Wednesday a few days earlier, was handed the reins on a caretaker basis. He somewhat reluctantly accepted the position on a permanent basis a few days later, and the former Blackburn Rovers manager merely tinkered with the side to ensure the Owls stayed away from the relegation places.

The club now seemed to be at a crossroads as the promising young side of the mid-1960s had not really matured as Wednesday would have hoped. It was obvious that reinforcements were required if the club was to avoid a flirt with relegation. However, although only minimal recruitment took place in the summer of 1968, everything in the garden seemed rosy as the Owls side made a great start to the season with up-and-coming forward Jack Whitham grabbing ten goals in the first fourteen games of the season, including a treble on an unforgettable Hillsborough afternoon in August when newly crowned European champions Manchester United rolled into town with the likes of George Best and Bobby Charlton in their ranks. Over 51,000 packed into the ground and witnessed a truly astonishing game – believed by many to be the greatest match ever seen at the stadium – as the Owls recovered from a 4-2 deficit to register an thrilling 5-4 win. Typically for Wednesday, a few days later the club was humiliated down at Exeter City, losing 3-1 in the League Cup! The Owls remained in the top half of the division until the end of the year, but the now all-too-familiar post-Christmas slump kicked in, not helped by the loss of top scorer Whitham to injury, and Wednesday won just one solitary game from Boxing Day until the end of the season.

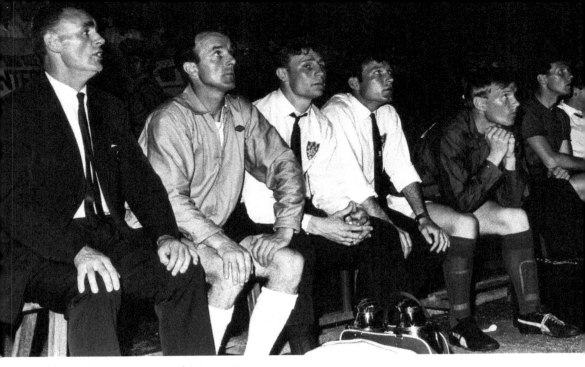

Above: Post-season tour of Asia, 1966.

Below: The 1966 FA Cup homecoming.

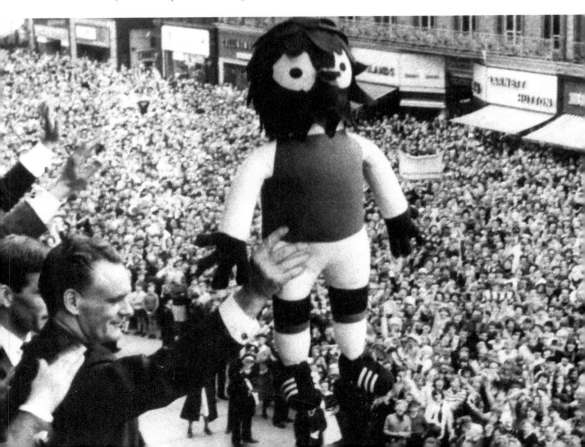

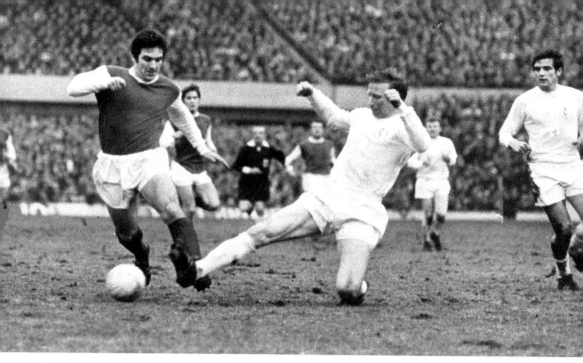

Above: Wednesday *v.* Leeds United, 1969 FA Cup tie.

Below: Don Megson testimonial including Bobby Moore and Martin Peters.

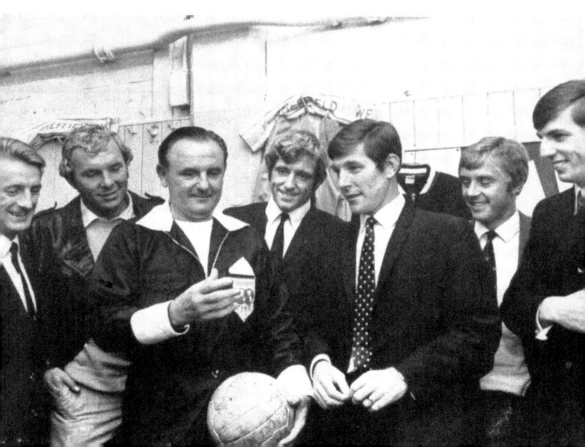

That terrible sequence included a 5-0 home thrashing by Arsenal in March 1969, which proved the final match in charge for manager Marshall. It was obvious that all was not well behind the scenes as several players had submitted transfer requests, and the apparent disharmony looked like a major factor in the run of poor results. The Owls boss had also discovered that the board of directors did not intend to renew his contract in the summer, so the home loss to the Gunners proved the straw that broke the camel's back – secretary Eric Taylor took temporary charge until the end of the season. In fact, the Owls were still without a permanent manager when they stunned the football world by paying Aberdeen £100,000 for highly rated midfielder Tommy Craig – a British record for a teenager. The youngster made his debut in the final game of the season – a 0-0 Hillsborough stalemate with Tottenham Hotspur – but unfortunately for Craig, and Wednesday, his arrival coincided with an awful period in the Owls' history, which saw them tumble down the leagues within a handful of seasons, all the way to the bottom of the old Third Division.

Their eventual fate seemed a million miles away when the Owls appointed manager Danny Williams in July 1969. The Rotherham-born Williams was one of the most sought-after managers in English football, not only leading Swindon Town to the Third Division title but also beating Arsenal at Wembley to lift the Football League Cup. His appointment was seen as coup, but his first act was to sell unsettled forward Jim McCalliog to Wolves and, coupled with the earlier departure of John Ritchie (sold back to Stoke City by Eric Taylor for a club record £70,000), it was obvious that the Owls went into the new season somewhat short of firepower. In addition, long-serving club stalwarts John Fantham, Don Megson and Gerry Young were all in the twilight of their careers, and it must quickly have dawned on the new boss that it would take a Herculean effort to get the Owls back into the higher reaches of First Division.

Wednesday started the 1969/70 season with a trio of consecutive defeats. Despite then posting back-to-back wins immediately afterwards, the club quickly slipped down into the lower reaches of the League. A run of six straight defeats in the period up to the Christmas fixtures duly dumped Wednesday onto the bottom rung of the table. A mini-revival in February subsequently gave Owls fans genuine hope as three wins in a row dragged Wednesday clear. That little run of form came after the Owls had been humiliated in the FA Cup, when minnows Scunthorpe United, with Kevin Keegan in their ranks, won 2-1 at Hillsborough in the fourth round, watched by a stunned crowd of over 38,000. It was obvious that the players brought into the club by Danny Williams were not of the standard required, with signings from lower Scottish League football (Willie Lawson) never really expected to 'cut the mustard' in the top flight of English soccer. As the gloom descended on Hillsborough, the team gave their fans hope of avoiding the drop after a home win over Nottingham Forest left the Owls two places away from danger. However, it was a false dawn, as the proverbial wheels then fell off with four defeats on the bounce leaving Wednesday in twenty-second spot, with only two games remaining to save themselves. A terrific draw at Old Trafford – the Owls recovering from a 2-0 deficit – still left the matter unresolved. The football gods seem to be aiding Wednesday as they went into the final game, at home to Manchester City, knowing a win would be enough to avoid the dreaded drop.

The Lancashire visitors had one eye on their forthcoming appearance in the final of the European Cup Winners' Cup, and it looked an ideal opportunity for the much criticised home players to lift their game and ensure top-flight football remained in the city, United having been relegated two seasons earlier. Wednesday fans turned out in force to cheer their heroes on, with Hillsborough hosting the biggest crowd of the season (45,258), but Manchester City had not read the script and despite a goal from Tony Coleman, it was Wednesday who joined Sunderland (managed by old boss Brown) through the trapdoor, losing 2-1. The Owls lost twenty-five of their forty-two League games and it was a clear that a lack of firepower had cost them dearly – Jack Whitham, who crucially missed the majority of the season because of injury, finished top scorer with only eight League goals.

FROM BAD TO WORSE

In the aftermath of relegation, Wednesday made positive noises about bouncing straight back. This seemed a possibility when Danny Williams persuaded two players, Sammy Todd and John Sissons, to drop down a division to sign for the Owls. The mercurial talents of Tommy Craig were still at the club's disposal, while highly rated full-back Wilf Smith and young attacker Mick Prendergast seemed to form the nucleus of a promotion-challenging side. The harsh realities of life outside of the top division were shown on the opening day, however, when only just over 17,000 watched the 1-0 win over visitors Charlton Athletic. In fact, average crowds would drop by an astonishing 10,568 from the club's final season in the First Division. Sadly for the fans who remained loyal, the 1970/71 season was not a vintage one, as Wednesday failed to mount any challenge for promotion and in fact ended the season in the bottom half of the division. One of the first acts of the new campaign was the sale of full-back Wilf Smith for a record fee, and the Owls would rely heavily on the inexperienced Prendergast, who quickly became a fan favourite for his goals. The season was not helped by a flu epidemic that swept through the club and, as fortunes waned, it became obvious that manager Williams was not the man to stop the rot. The Owls board dispensed with his services on somewhat acrimonious terms in January 1971, with the club treading water in thirteenth place. His replacement was certainly a popular choice among supporters as former battering ram centre-forward Derek Dooley was handed the hot seat. Despite the mounting financial problems – Wednesday reporting a large loss for the year ending May 1971 – Dooley would vastly improve the side during his first eighteen months in charge, signing the likes of Willie Henderson, David Sunley and Brian Joicey. His first act was to ensure the Owls were not sucked into relegation danger at the foot of the Second Division and this was achieved with a finishing position of fifteenth, despite Wednesday failing to win any of their final seven games. The final home match of the campaign also provided a shock for the club's hierarchy as only 9,720 fans attended the 2-1 defeat to Sunderland, which was the lowest recorded official gate for a Wednesday home game at the time. The slump in support was even more remarkable as twelve days earlier, 47,592 had watched the Steel City derby end 0-0 at Hillsborough.

The 1971/72 season saw Dooley's side slowly emerge from the ashes of the 1970 relegation team. The campaign was not without its trauma, though. Wednesday were beaten 5-1 in their opening home match, lost their first four games and were humiliated 5-0 at Carlisle United in the League Cup. Sixteen League goals from new man Joicey would help steady the ship, and the Owls eventually finished the season in fourteenth place, just five points off the drop. One of the few highlights was a return visit to Hillsborough by Pelé and his Santos team, which attracted by far the biggest crowd of the season. Just under 37,000 attended despite the game being played

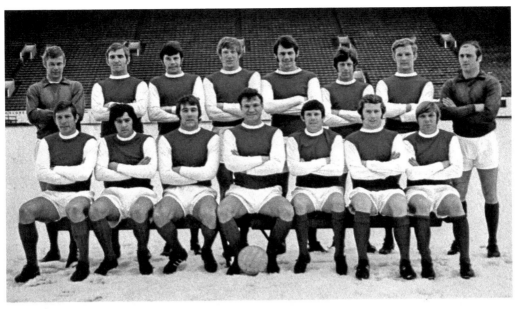

LEFT TO RIGHT

STANDING
P. GRUMMITT, H. WILCOCKSON, C. PROPHETT, S. ELLIS, A. WARBOYS, K. BURTON, J. WHITHAM, P. SPRINGETT

SEATED
D. MEGSON, S. DOWNES, W. SMITH, G. YOUNG, J. SINCLAIR, T. CRAIG, T. COLEMAN

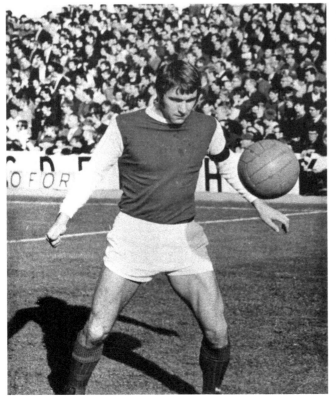

Above: Team group, 1969/70.

Left: Left-back Wilf Smith, *c.* 1970.

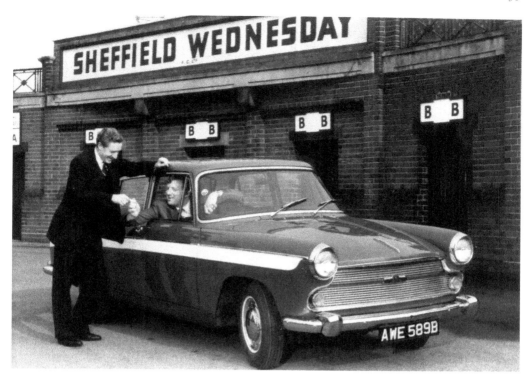

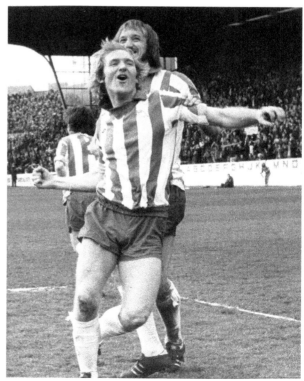

Above: Manager Dooley and his sponsored club car.

Right: Escape from relegation, April 1974.

on a mid-week afternoon – sick notes, dentist appointments and absent schoolboys were probably at a yearly high on that day! After three somewhat depressing campaigns, Wednesday fans had much to enjoy in the following season. Dooley's side played an attractive brand of football, which resulted in a flirt with promotion and an exciting run in the FA Cup. The Owls also welcomed back both Peter Swan and David Layne, who had seen their life bans quashed by the authorities, and the former was in the side that started the season with a 3-0 home win over Fulham, watched by a highly encouraging crowd in excess of 23,000. The Owls would win seven of their opening eleven games to top the table, before over 30,000 saw Burnley win 1-0 at Hillsborough, knocking them off their lofty perch. The Owls remained in contention for the top two places until well into the New Year, while a run to the last sixteen of the FA Cup commenced with a home win over Fulham to set up a meeting with top-flight Crystal Palace. After two draws, the tie went to a second replay at Villa Park, where Owls fans dominated the crowd and watched their side register a famous extra-time win, thanks to a treble from Brian Joicey. It was again London opposition in the fifth round, but in front of almost 47,000 it was Chelsea who went through, recovering from an early goal to win 2-1. It was then back to the bread and butter of the League, with fifteen-year-old rookie goalkeeper Peter Fox becoming the club's all-time youngest player when he was pressed into action for the 2-0 home win over Orient in March 1973. The Owls' final position at the season's end – tenth – was actually the lowest they had been all season. Despite less than 9,000 fans attending the final home fixture – setting a new low crowd mark – there was genuine hope that Dooley's side would be real promotion contenders in 1973/74.

For a variety of reasons, the club subsequently experienced a dreadful three seasons, which saw them slide out of the Second Division and almost drop into the Fourth, against a backdrop of near financial ruin. The Owls made a poor start to the season, despite the arrival of experienced centre-half Ken Knighton, and a run of injuries and sickness meant that the side was struggling at the wrong end of the table as Christmas approached – early-season problems included a 8-2 League Cup mauling at Queens Park Rangers.

Against that background of mounting debts, manager Dooley seemed to be dealing manfully with the job at hand, but on Christmas Eve 1973, the world of football was shocked when the Owls board, led by new chairman Matt Sheppard, sensationally sacked the club's manager. The actual timing of the decision led to huge criticism of the Owls from fans and the media, and it is not surprising to learn that Dooley did not set foot inside Hillsborough for almost twenty years following the insensitive dismissal. It was at this point that the club's history could have taken an upward turn, as both Brian Clough and Ron Atkinson applied for the vacant post, but the Owls instead plumped for little-known coach Steve Burtenshaw, who had never held a managerial post before! Sadly, the new manager would simply be out of his depth as a veritable 'fire sale' took place at Hillsborough, with the likes of Sissons and goalie Peter Grummitt headed for the exit doors. A 8-0 defeat at Jack Charlton's Middlesbrough on the penultimate Saturday of the season meant the Owls had to win their final game at home to Bolton Wanderers to avoid a second relegation in four years. A goal from Knighton did secure the vital two points, but unfortunately it only postponed the inevitable, and the 1974/75 season proved to be one of the worst in their entire history. Cost-cutting measures and increased prices meant that the Owls went into the new season with just 3,000 season tickets holders, and the stay-away fans were proven correct as Wednesday quickly slipped to the bottom of the League and exited the League Cup at Scunthorpe United.

Apart from a brief flurry in late autumn, when loan forward Eric McMordie netted six goals in nine games, the Owls would remain at the foot of the table, and incredibly failed to win any of their final seventeen games of the campaign, suffering relegation on April Fool's Day 1975 after losing at Nottingham Forest – by this time fan favourite Tommy Craig had also been sold, moving to First Division Newcastle United. An even worse statistic showed that Wednesday did not even score for a staggering fourteen hours and ten minutes before Brian Joicey grabbed a last-minute equaliser in the home game against Oxford United. The leveller was celebrated by the faithful – crowds had now fallen well under five figures – as home fans had waited since before Christmas for a goal at Hillsborough! Wednesday finished the season with their lowest-ever points tally (twenty-one), recorded only five wins and scored only twenty-nine goals to finish eleven points adrift at the bottom. It was certainly a season that fans would not forget in a hurry, sadly for all the wrong reasons.

Unfortunately, the club's first-ever season in the Third Division did little to lift the air of despondency around Hillsborough. Although Wednesday fans travelled in huge numbers to many grounds that the Owls had never visited, those supporters failed to witness a single away win as their club struggled through the entire 1975/76 season at the wrong end of the table. In addition to events on the pitch, Wednesday continued to incur huge losses in their annual accounts, and on a day-to-day basis were almost at breaking point, with their increasing bank overdraft a constant worry. Several playing and non-playing staff were made redundant, including the chief scout and physiotherapist, and the club announced that no money would be available for incoming transfers, Wednesday having to rely on home-grown players from a youth system that was also being run on a shoestring budget. There is no doubt that this was the lowest point in the Owls' long history, and it also spelt the end for beleaguered manager Burtenshaw, who departed in October 1975 after Wednesday had recorded just two League wins. New chairman Bert McGee wielded the axe, and it was his promotion to the chair and the appointment of new manager Len Ashurst that would finally lay the foundations needed to lift the Owls from the doldrums.

Ashurst arrived after leaving Gillingham – Wednesday eventually paying compensation to the Kent club after several months of legal arguments – and quickly instilled some confidence in the side to at least show a slight improvement in results. He hit the headlines in January 1976 after his coach, ex-Marine Tony Toms, took the players onto the moors for a night of survival training! It's not known whether the two were connected, but a month later the Owls had two matches postponed as an outbreak of influenza hit the playing staff! A late run of consecutive home successes lifted Wednesday to the brink of safety, and the relegation issue went down to a rearranged home game against Southend United at Hillsborough, played after the other teams had finished their campaigns. As is usually the case, Wednesday fans came out in force to help their side in a moment of crisis (the 25,000-plus crowd more than twice the seasonal average), and the Owls duly secured the one point minimum required as first-half goals from Mick Prendergast and Eric Potts took Wednesday to a 2-1 win and a second last-day survival in just three years.

Happily, Ashurst's first full season in charge provided some respite for Wednesday fans, as a morale-boosting pre-season win in the Shipp Cup tournament and giant-killing success against Wolves in the League Cup gave the Owls a flying start. The emergence of attacker Rodger Wylde was a big factor, with the livewire striker grabbing twenty-one League goals (the first Owls player to pass the twenty League goal mark since David Layne thirteen years earlier).

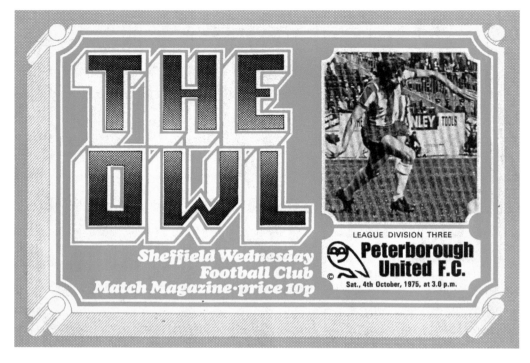

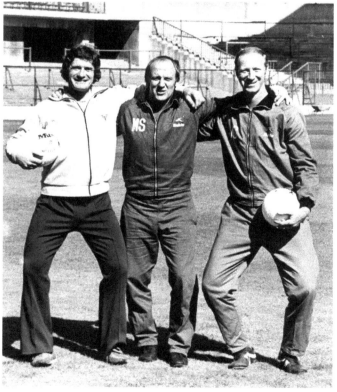

Above: A colourful 1975 matchday programme.

Left: Manager Jack Charlton, assistant Maurice Setters and physio Tony Toms.

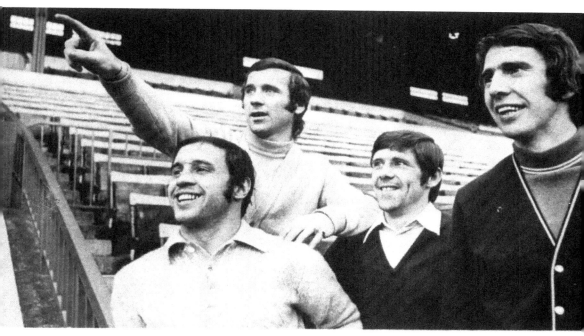

Above: Willie Henderson, Tommy Craig, Jackie Sinclair and Jim Craig, 1972.

Below: Centre-forward Andy McCulloch heads for goal at Bristol Rovers in 1980.

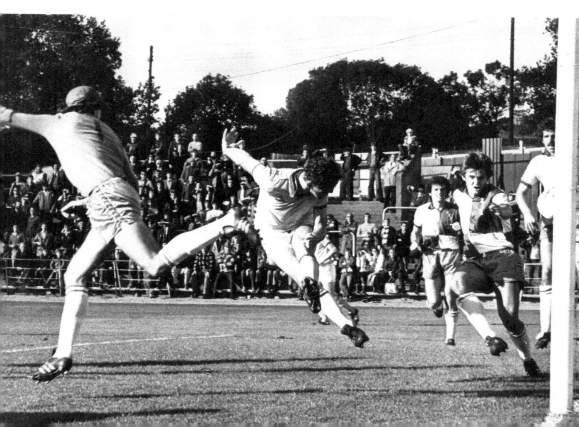

Wednesday would spend the vast majority of the season in the top half of the table, finishing eighth in the division. His partnership with Tommy Tynan was arguably the best during the whole decade and the Owls rose as high as fourth place during the season. The club's finances were also starting to improve, although losses continued, and there seemed genuine reason to believe that the tide had turned and that Len Ashurst would be the man to get the club back up the leagues. Unfortunately, with Wednesday you can usually rely upon them to do exactly the opposite of what is expected. The start of the 1977/78 campaign proved an example of this as the side suffered a torturous start and sat rock bottom after ten League games with a paltry five points!

THE ARRIVAL OF JACK &
THE SLEEPING GIANT AWAKENS

Despite the apparent progress made under Ashurst in overall terms, he could not hope to survive such a terrible run and was duly shown the door after a 2-1 defeat at Preston North End in October 1977. Wednesday therefore entertained Chesterfield at Hillsborough a week later with caretaker Ken Knighton in charge, although all eyes in the ground were on former World Cup winner Jack Charlton, who, it was rumoured, was considering the vacant position. Due to the subsequent positive feedback received by 'Big Jack' from the Wednesday fans, he decided to accept the offer and became the club's fourteenth manager. The first job for the new incumbent was to make Wednesday difficult to beat, although his first game in charge was a 2-1 defeat at Exeter City. As autumn turned to winter, Wednesday remained at the wrong end of the Third Division and, for some fans, reached absolute rock bottom when Northern Premier League Wigan Athletic dumped the Owls out of the FA Cup after winning 1-0 at their old Springfield Park ground. After being a victim of 'giant killing', the Owls started to pick up results. By January 1978 they had moved out of the bottom four places and would end the season in a relatively comfortable lower mid-table position. The season also saw the first real signs of financial recovery – the Owls actually paid a fee for a player (£45,000 to Shrewsbury Town for Brian Hornsby) – and figures would later show, thanks to the new lottery run by ex-player Dennis Woodhead, that Wednesday registered an astonishing profit of almost £130,000 for the financial year ending 31 May 1978.

It was clear that the stringent cost-cutting measures, combined with changes at boardroom level, had saved the club from financial ruin, and the side enjoyed a stress free 1978/79 season, drawing a club record nineteen games to finish in fourteenth place for the second consecutive campaign. The season will always be remembered for the FA Cup, as the Owls battled through to the third round, overcoming both Scunthorpe United and Tranmere Rovers in home replays, to set up a tie with Arsenal, who had reached the previous season's final. On a snowy afternoon at Hillsborough, the teams battled out a 1-1 draw, watched by over 33,000 fans, and were a whisker away from causing a major upset in the Highbury replay as a Rodger Wylde goal put the Owls ahead only for the Gunners to grab a last-minute equaliser. Due to the inclement weather conditions, the venue for the third game (in those days all second replays were staged at neutral venues) in the saga was played at Leicester City's Filbert Street ground, which boasted a weather beating pitch cover. This finished 2-2 and the tie became the centre of national interest as Wednesday then shared six goals with the Londoners in the fourth game. The fifth meeting proved a bridge too far for the plucky Wednesday side, and it ended 2-0 to Arsenal, with the tie entering history as the third longest ever played in the tournament. The tie certainly returned a lot of pride to the minds of Wednesday fans, and before the end of the campaign the Owls bought winger Terry Curran from top-flight Southampton, equalling their ten-year-old transfer record in the process. The likes of Mel Sterland, Kevin Taylor and Mark Smith were also breaking through from a now flourishing youth setup and Wednesday finally looked set to start the long road back to the higher echelons of the English game.

The summer of 1979 saw Jack Charlton sign Andy McCulloch, Jeff King and Ian Mellor, and his side opened the League campaign with a tremendous 3-0 win against neighbours Barnsley. However, Wednesday duly lost their opening League home game by the same score and, for the first half of the season, were in the shadow of Sheffield United, who raced away at the top of the table. The season would famously turn for both city clubs on Boxing Day 1979, when a record crowd for the division – just under 50,000 – packed into Hillsborough to see the Owls thrash their neighbours 4-0 in a game that has entered club folklore as the 'Boxing Day Massacre'. Despite losing their next home game, it would be the blue-and-white side of Sheffield that soared up the table, as United headed in the opposite direction, with a sixteen-game unbeaten run pushing the Owls to the brink of promotion. During that run, Mark Smith netted his eleventh goal from the penalty spot to set a new club record, and crowds were returning to Hillsborough, with several games nudging over the 20,000 mark. The fight for promotion went down to a permutation of three from four as Grimsby Town, Blackburn Rovers and Chesterfield joined Wednesday in striving for a place in the Second Division. A subsequent 2-1 win at Blackburn, in front of several thousand travelling Owls fans, put the club on the brink and, despite losing 1-0 at Exeter City four days later, it was Wednesday who claimed the third promotion slot after Chesterfield were beaten at Millwall. Promotion could be celebrated a week later when over 32,000 attended the final game of the season against Carlisle United, and it seemed like the vast majority invaded the pitch at the final whistle as Wednesday fans said goodbye to the dark days of the 1970s.

The Owls went into the new season on the back of record profits and started in fine style, beating Newcastle United on the opening day of the League campaign and overcoming Sheffield United, over two legs, in the first round of the League Cup. The club's determination to make an impact in the division was shown in October 1980, when they splashed out a club record £250,000 to make Yugoslavian midfielder Ante Miročević their first ever 'foreign' signing. This was after a riot by Owls fans at Oldham Athletic had tarnished the club's image and led to several games being held at Hillsborough where all standing areas were closed. The club was also handed down a hefty fine and Wednesday fans were banned for four away games, although a few hundred simply paid on the gate and a huge roar could be heard from the banned supporters when the Owls scored! In the League, Wednesday enjoyed a great season and remained unbeaten at home until early January. They were in contention for promotion until early April before losing six of their final seven games to slide down to tenth place. However, Charlton's side were clearly a force to be reckoned with, and the addition

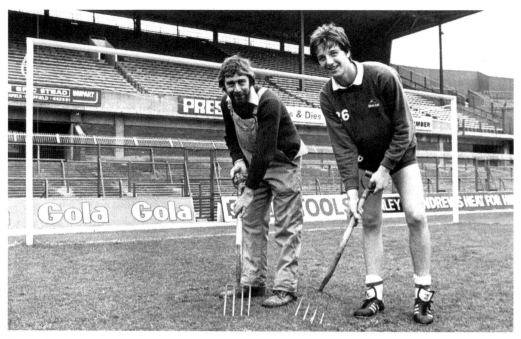

Groundsman Dave Barber and a teenage John Pearson, *c.* 1980.

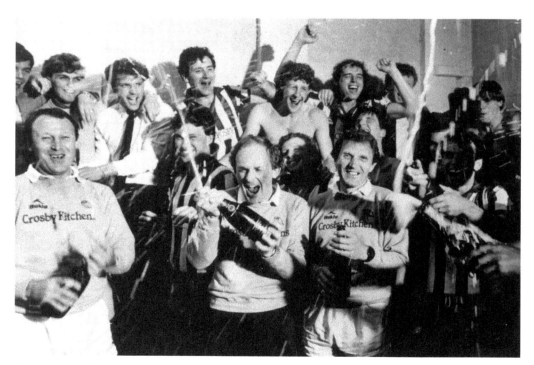

Promotion, 1984.

of Gary Bannister and Gary Megson, in the summer of 1981 meant that they were rated as promotion favourites by the pundits. They duly started the season like a 'house on fire' and won their first four games to top the table. A mixed bag of results followed, and a bad winter saw the fixture list decimated, but the Owls stormed back to sit in the third promotion place with only five games remaining. The prize was there to be lost by Wednesday and, agonisingly, that's what they did. A 4-0 defeat at Watford was followed by two draws against Chelsea and neighbours Rotherham United, before a 3-1 defeat at Bolton Wanderers ended their hopes. On the final day of the season, the Owls beat Norwich City, who had pinched that third promotion place, with Gary Bannister scoring his twenty-second goal of the campaign. Wednesday's only consolation was that if three points for a win had been introduced a year later then it would have been Jack Charlton's men who were promoted!

The summer of 1982 saw the somewhat acrimonious departure of fan favourite Terry Curran to Sheffield United, while vastly experienced centre-half Mick Lyons joined from Everton. Wednesday made another great start with the home success over Bolton Wanderers, notable as teenager John Pearson scored after just thirteen seconds, the quickest goal ever recorded at Hillsborough. However, it would be Cup football that would dominate the season as the Owls reached the League Cup quarter-finals for the first time (losing at Arsenal) and recorded wins over Southend United, Torquay United, Cambridge United and Burnley (5-0 in a replay on an unforgettable Hillsborough evening) to book a Highbury meeting with top-flight strugglers Brighton Hove Albion in the semi-finals of the FA Cup. On a red-hot afternoon in North London, the Owls went behind. A last-ever goal in Wednesday colours from Miročević (he was released at the end of the season) levelled matters only for the Sussex club to end hopes of Wembley as Michael Robinson scored a late winner. The League campaign proved somewhat disappointing in the end, despite finishing in sixth place, and the end of the season saw the departure of manager Charlton, who decided to take a break from football after six successful seasons with Wednesday.

THE ARRIVAL OF 'BIG RON'

After failing to gain the services of locally born manager Graham Taylor, the Owls instead appointed Notts County boss and former Wednesday winger Howard Wilkinson to the vacant position. The Sheffield-born Wilkinson quickly set about revamping the side with Andy McCulloch and Bob Bolder departing, the latter to European champions Liverpool, and Imre Varadi, Lawrie Madden and Martin Hodge arriving. The club's style of play also altered, as Wilkinson introduced a direct, high-tempo game to the Hillsborough faithful, and those fans were delighted as the club made a remarkable start to the 1983/84 season, failing to taste defeat in the first eighteen games of the campaign – a club record. The run included progress to the latter stages of the League Cup and ended with a single-goal defeat at Crystal Palace on the final Saturday of November. Such a remarkable start meant the Owls were firm favourites to reclaim their top-flight place, lost in 1970, and Wednesday indeed remained in the divisional top two for the whole season, clinching promotion thanks to a Mel Sterland

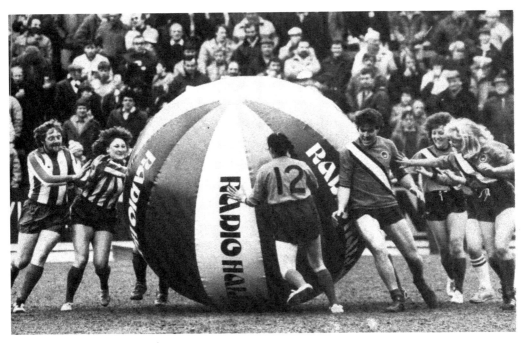

The half-time Radio Hallam ball, *c.* 1985.

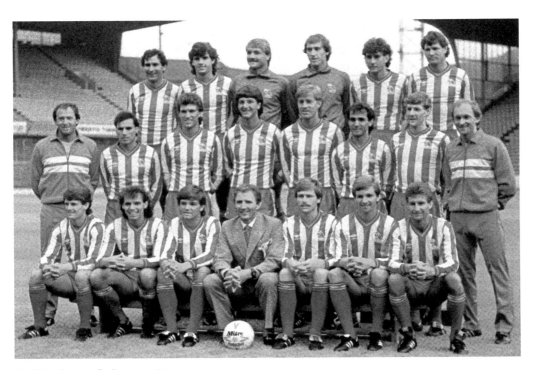

Back in the top flight, 1984/85.

penalty, ironically against a Crystal Palace side that ended their great start to the season five months earlier. A late loss of form saw the title lost to Chelsea on the final day of the season, but this mattered little to Wednesday fans with First Division soccer already secured. Top scorer, for a third season running, was Gary Bannister with twenty-two goals in all competitions; new strike partner, Imre Varadi, chipped in with nineteen strikes. Mick Lyons and Lawrie Madden proved rocks at the heart of the defence, with Martin Hodge in fine form between the sticks. The Owls also enjoyed a remarkable season in cup-tie football, reaching the last eight in both domestic competitions. The League Cup run ended in a replay defeat at Anfield, after almost 50,000 watched a thrilling 2-2 draw at Hillsborough. Cameras televised the first-ever live game from Hillsborough when Southampton held the Owls to a 0-0 draw in the sixth round – the Saints winning 5-1 in the replay.

The summer of 1984 saw the surprise departure of top scorer Gary Bannister to fellow First Division side Queens Park Rangers, while Gary Megson also left for new pastures. Arriving was target man Lee Chapman and winger Brian Marwood, and Wednesday enjoyed a terrific start to life back with the big boys, with over 30,000 watching Varadi net a wonder strike in a 3-1 opening-day home win over Nottingham Forest. A famous victory at Liverpool followed, and a 5-0 home success over Leicester City, in October 1984, took the Owls to the dizzy heights of second place in the League. Despite slowly dropping down the table, Wednesday still ended the season in a highly satisfactory eighth position, just a handful of points off the top five. They again reached the last eight of the League Cup, bowing out at Chelsea after the Londoners had turned a 3-0 half-time deficit at Hillsborough into a 4-3 lead, before Mel Sterland famously netted a last-minute penalty to force extra time and a subsequent replay. A year after losing Gary Bannister, Wednesday again had to say goodbye to their top marksman – twenty-one-goal Imre Varadi – although the club record fee of £285,000 from West Bromwich Albion was some consolation. Forward Garry Thompson duly arrived to fill Varadi's boots, and the Owls again made a big impression in their second season back in the First Division, sitting second in the table in the early weeks of the season and seemingly offering the only challenge to runaway leaders Manchester United. The Owls were, in fact, the first team to lower the colours of Ron Atkinson's United side, winning 1-0 in front of over 48,000 on an unforgettable Hillsborough afternoon, while later in the season the emergence of former non-League player Carl Shutt helped propel the Owls to an FA Cup semi-final meeting with Everton at Villa Park. Unfortunately, despite an equalising goal from Shutt, dreams of Wembley were again put on hold as a late goal from Graeme Sharp sent Everton through to an all-Merseyside final. Back in the League, the Owls finished strongly, winning five of their final six games to clinch fifth place behind a Manchester United side that had travelled in the opposite direction!

With manager Wilkinson, assistant Peter Eustace and physiotherapist Alan Smith all tied to new long-term contracts, further progress seemed assured, and the Owls added to their ranks with the signing of highly rated eighteen-year-old attacker David Hirst from Barnsley. The summer also saw work undertaken on the long-awaited roofing of Hillsborough's Spion Kop, which was opened and packed by Owls fans for the 2-2 draw with Everton in August 1986 – the new structure was officially opened by HM Queen Elizabeth II in December of the same year. On the pitch, Wednesday spent the first half of the season in the top half of the First Division table, sitting in fifth place prior to the Christmas programme of fixtures. During the first set of games, Coventry City 'keeper Steve Ogrizovic became the only custodian to score

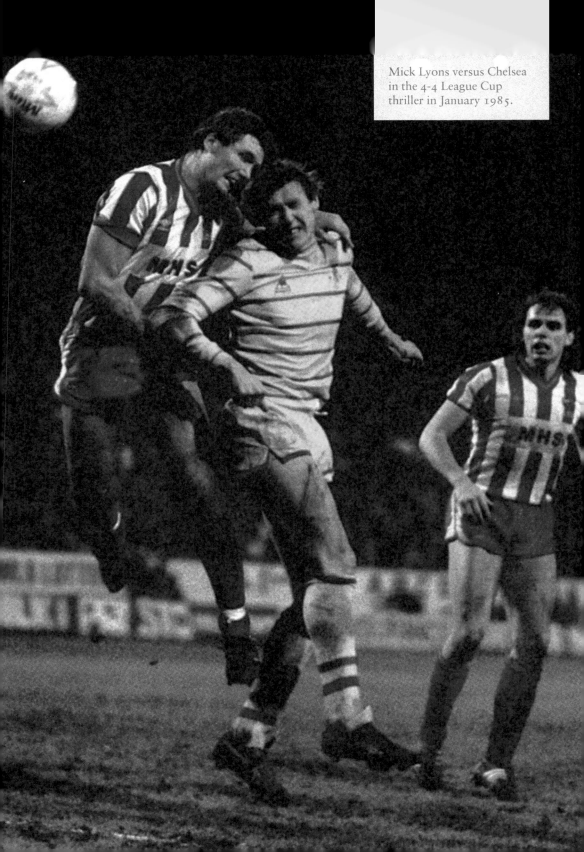

against the Owls when he bounced a long punt upfield and over a startled Martin Hodge in the home net. Former dustman Colin Walker became the only Wednesday player to score a hat-trick as a substitute, achieving the rare feat in a League Cup tie at Stockport County. However, the side then hit the proverbial buffers and won only a handful of games to slip dramatically down the table – an FA Cup run to the quarter-finals somewhat masking the bad run in League football. A terrific 7-1 home win over Queens Park Rangers steadied the ship and Wednesday finished just below mid-table, with a need for reinforcements in the summer clearly a top priority. However, the club refused to break their wage structure and Wilkinson would be left frustrated as various moves in the transfer market came to nothing. It would be that inability to compete in the transfer market that eventually saw Wilkinson tender his resignation just over a year later. The Owls did finish the 1987/88 season in a safe mid-table position, ending with an embarrassing home thrashing by champions Liverpool, and a four-game FA Cup marathon with Everton grabbing the majority of the headlines – Wednesday drawing three times before a spectacular 5-0 collapse in the third replay at Hillsborough. The squad was further weakened by the sale of forward Lee Chapman, and the Owls went into the next season with virtually no forwards in their squad, Mel Sterland filling in for several games. After a 1-0 win over Aston Villa in early October 1988, the Owls' boss tendered his resignation, joining a Leeds United side that he would lead to the top-flight title just over three years later – comparisons with the departure of Harry Catterick, over twenty-five years earlier, all too obvious.

The search then began for a new manager, but after publicly being rebuffed by several targets, they instead appointed caretaker boss Peter Eustace to the role. It proved a disastrous decision as the new incumbent lasted only 109 days as results deteriorated and disharmony in the dressing room led to transfer requests from various players. The whole sorry episode inevitably ended in February 1989, as Eustace departed Hillsborough with the Owls in relegation trouble and seemingly trying to stay in the division on a shoestring budget. What happened next was a big shock to Owls fans, and in the long run would lead to one of the greatest periods in the Owls' long history. The new manager was none other than 'Big Ron' Atkinson, who had enjoyed successful spells at West Bromwich Albion and Manchester United while cultivating a somewhat flamboyant reputation. One of his first acts was to allow Mel Sterland to leave for Glasgow Rangers before breaking the Owls' transfer record to spend £750,000 on midfield dynamo Carlton Palmer. Forward Steve Whitton also arrived, but the next few months would be dominated by other events, as the tragedy at the April 1989 FA Cup semi-final led to ninety-six deaths and saw the indefinite closure of the Leppings Lane end of the ground. The Owls' fixture list was also rearranged, and it was on the final Saturday of the season that a goal from Whitton secured safety for Wednesday and relegation for their opponents, Middlesbrough.

Despite initially only joining the Owls on a short-term basis, Atkinson was persuaded to sign a new one-year deal prior to the final game of the season, and Wednesday fans had genuine hope that the 1989/90 campaign would see a revival in the club's fortunes. The arrival of Big Ron seemed to revitalise the career of David Hirst, and his partnership with new arrival Dalian Atkinson proved a potent force in the new campaign, with the duo netting thirty-one times. Unfortunately, an unexpectedly turbulent start proved a shock to fans as the Owls won only one of their opening eleven League games to slide to the bottom of the division. A club record

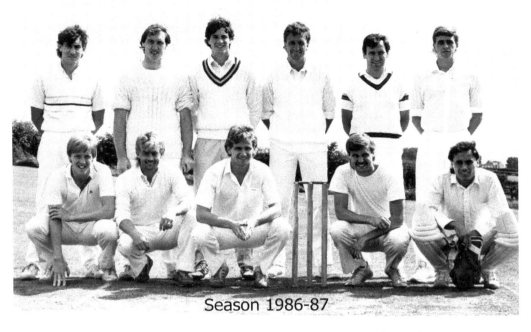

Season 1986-87

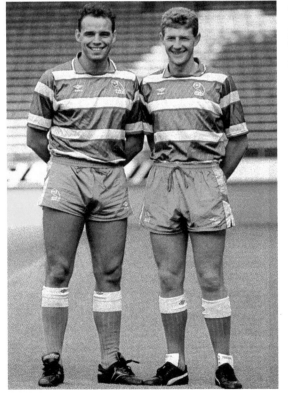

Above: Anyone for cricket?

Right: Mel Sterland and Nigel Worthington model the new 1988 away kit.

away win – 8-0 at Aldershot in the League Cup – proved some consolation but the hoped for revival did take place after the signings of John Sheridan, Phil King and Roland Nilsson. A new expansive game delighted the purists and, by early spring, Wednesday were seemingly heading towards a comfortable mid-table finish. Sadly, the side then just ran out of both luck and confidence and found themselves needing a solitary point to preserve their status on the final day. It was not to be, however, and a 3-0 reverse at home to Nottingham Forest, combined with a win for relegation rivals Luton Town, sent the Owls back into the Second Division.

ANOTHER GOLDEN AGE

The overwhelming feeling among Owls fans was one of pure shock, as Atkinson's side had played some highly attractive football and literally fitted the old adage that they seemed too good to go down. The promotion of neighbours United, literally replacing Wednesday in the top flight, increased the disappointment, but with Atkinson committed to remaining at Hillsborough, he set about reshaping the side. His recruitment was helped by the club record £1.7 million sale of Dalian Atkinson to Spanish football, with Paul Williams and Danny Wilson brought in. What followed was one of the most exciting seasons in modern times, as a swashbuckling Wednesday side not only took the club straight back up but also secured the Owls' only domestic cup since before the Second World War.

Thousands of Wednesday fans travelled to see an opening-day win at Ipswich Town. David Hirst then grabbed four goals as Hull City were defeated at Hillsborough. Wednesday would not be beaten until late October 1990 and, combined with runs in both League and FA Cup, remained in the divisional top three for the vast majority of the campaign. A win at First Division Coventry City secured a first-ever League Cup semi-final place, and Wednesday stunned another top-flight side, Chelsea, by winning 2-0 in London and 3-1 in Sheffield to book a Wembley place. After exiting the FA Cup at Cambridge United, Wednesday kept in the promotion hunt before the big day at the National Stadium. Wembley Way was a sea of blue and white for the final against Manchester United, and an unforgettable goal from John Sheridan, just before half-time, proved the winner, with Owls fans in raptures at the final whistle when captain Nigel Pearson lifted the trophy.

It was quickly back to League football for Wednesday, with the players parading the cup before fans at the home game against Leicester City. A crucial win against promotion rivals Notts County pushed the Owls even further towards regaining their First Division place, and this was duly achieved on another memorable Hillsborough evening as a brace from Hirst and a goal from Trevor Francis sealed a 3-1 win over Bristol City. The season ended on Oldham's infamous plastic pitch, Wednesday losing a two-goal lead to miss out on runners-up spot, but it had been a truly unforgettable season with David Hirst netting thirty-two goals in League and Cup football and ending his campaign with a call-up for the full England squad. A tremendous partnership with Paul Williams had contributed greatly to Hirst's goal tally, while inspirational captain Pearson not only lead the side but also chipped in with twelve goals himself. As with most successful teams, Wednesday had several players who were virtually

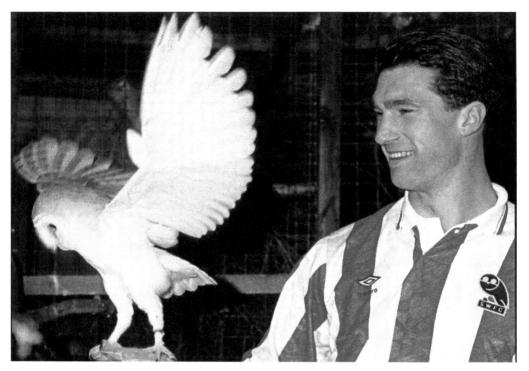

Club captain Nigel Pearson with a feathered friend, 1990.

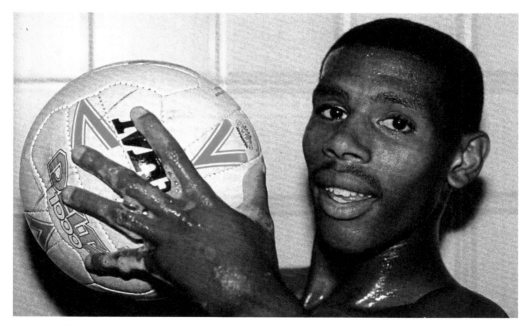

Match ball for Carlton Palmer *v.* Queens Park Rangers, 1991.

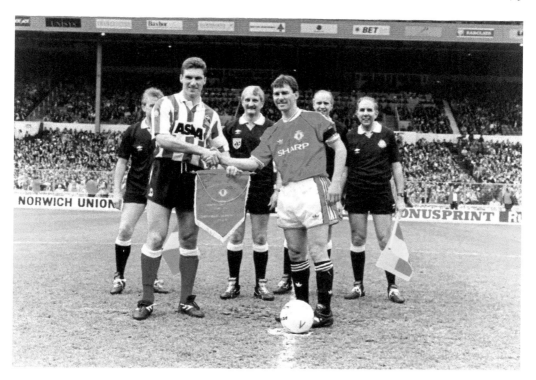

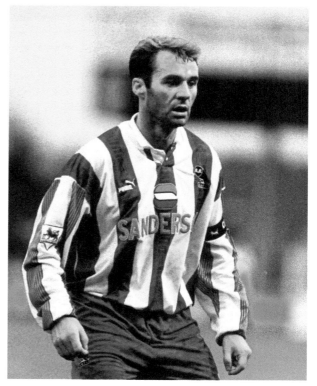

Above: Toss up before the 1991
League Cup final.

Right: The 1990s midfield maestro
John Sheridan.

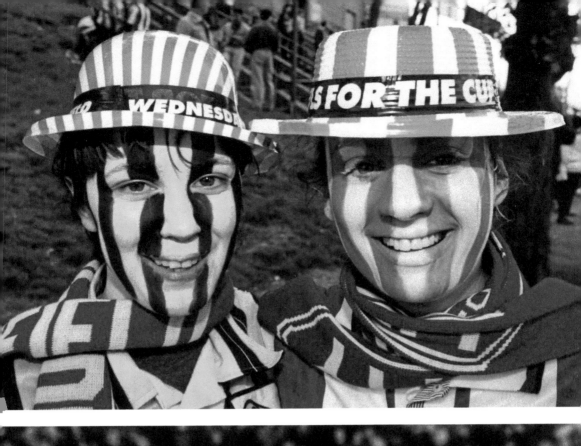
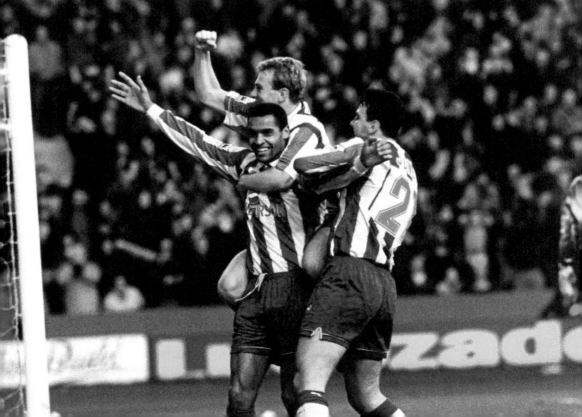

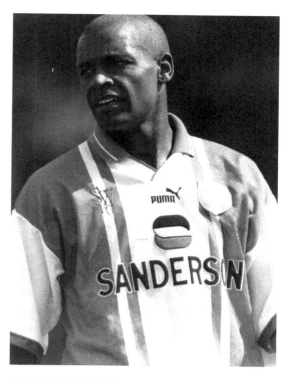

Opposite above: Wednesday at Wembley, 1993.

Opposite below: Players celebrate a goal against the Blades in January 1994.

Right above: Mark Bright (1992–96), 70 goals in 170 appearances.

Right below: Marc Degryse and Steve Nicol take a breather during training, 1995.

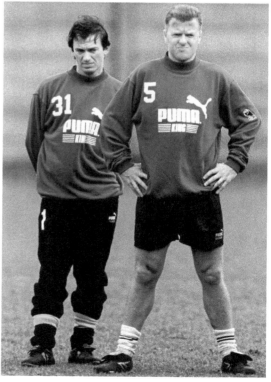

ever present, with the aforementioned Sheridan and Williams playing in all forty-six League fixtures, while Carlton Palmer missed only two of the sixty-one games played by the Owls in the season – unfortunately one of those was the Wembley final, after he was red carded in a League game at Portsmouth. The season also saw the reserve side lift the Central League title for the first time for thirty years, and the club's youth team were finalists in the prestigious FA Youth Cup for the first time.

The new season would be the most eagerly awaited for many a year, but before the new fixtures were even announced the club, and fans, were rocked when Ron Atkinson sensationally resigned to join Aston Villa, the club he had supported as a youngster. However, he was persuaded to change his mind by chairman Dave Richards, and his popularity rose even further as 'Big Ron' led the team around the city streets for a civic reception to mark their double success. Unfortunately, Atkinson then went from hero to villain as he made another U-turn, moving to Villa after all, to leave Owls fans hugely disappointed and somewhat furious with their former boss. Wednesday moved quickly to fill the void, appointing Trevor Francis as player-manager, and soon after the club broke the £1 million transfer barrier for the first time as England goalkeeper Chris Woods arrived from Glasgow Rangers.

The Football League fixture computer must have had a mischievous chip installed in that summer, as out popped Wednesday *v.* Aston Villa on the opening day. Atkinson received a 'red hot' reception from Owls fans still smarting from the manner of his departure. Two great goals from Hirst and Wilson looked set to give Wednesday the revenge that the supporters so craved, but it was 'Big Ron' who had the last laugh as his side recovered from two goals down to snatch all three points. Despite the disappointing start, the 1991/92 season would be another classic one as the Owls quickly moved into the top half of the table, helped by an amazing first-half hat-trick from Carlton Palmer against Queens Park Rangers, and they remained there for the rest of the campaign. The club's grip on the League Cup was ended by Southampton, in a replay at the Dell. Wednesday also exited the FA Cup, losing at home to Second Division Middlesbrough. However, the Owls' form in the bread and butter of the League was excellent, although a 6-1 televised home defeat to Leeds United – a game Wednesday tried to have called off due to a crippling injury list – was somewhat hard to swallow. In the same month, January 1992, boss Francis also gave a trial to former French international Eric Cantona, the fiery attacker playing in a six-a-side game at Sheffield Arena against Baltimore Blast. In hindsight, the subsequent 'non' from Cantona, after Francis asked to extend the trial as snowy weather meant he had not seen Cantona play on grass, changed the immediate histories of Wednesday, Leeds United and Manchester United, as a few months later he helped the West Yorkshire club to the title and became a modern-day legend at Old Trafford. Despite another shocking defeat, losing 7-1 at Arsenal after being all-square at seventy-two minutes, the Owls continued to mount an unexpected challenge for the title. It was only a last-minute goal from Mark Bright, for Crystal Palace, on the penultimate day of the season that ended hopes of a fifth top-flight championship. A considerable consolation was qualification for European football, for the first time since 1963, while a final position of third, just seven points behind first place, showed what a big impact Wednesday had made on their return to the top division.

With average crowds close to 30,000, there was even greater anticipation for the following season, as many pundits made the Owls favourites to lift the League title. The marquee signing of former England international Chris Waddle strengthened that view even further, and Wednesday made a good start in the inaugural season of the FA Premier League – the television rights having been sold to BSkyB for £304 million. Early progress was made in both the League and UEFA Cup, Luxembourg minnows Spora being beaten 10-2 on aggregate in the latter, although converted attacker Paul Warhurst almost lost his life on the pitch after swallowing his tongue in the 8-1 home rout. In the League, form was inconsistent and it was not until after the Christmas period that Wednesday started to show quite outstanding form. New signing Mark Bright was among the goals as the Owls won seven consecutive League games, the first time since the early 1950s, and Warhurst grabbed all the headlines as he simply could not stop scoring. An incredible 4-2 win at Blackburn Rovers virtually assured a Wembley place in the League Cup final, while a goal from Warhurst clinched an FA Cup semi-final meeting with the Blades. The most high-profile meeting of the two Sheffield rivals ended in a 2-1 win for Wednesday (Waddle and Bright), but the season would end somewhat anticlimactically as old foes Arsenal defeated the Owls in both Wembley finals. Despite a goal from John Harkes – becoming the first US player to score in a major English final – the Owls slipped to a 2-1 defeat to the Gunners in the League Cup final. They experienced real heartbreak in the final of the FA Cup after a goal from David Hirst had forced a Thursday night replay (the last one in the history of the tournament). A goal from Waddle levelled the scores on a rainy night in North London only for the Owls to cruelly succumb to a goal in the final minute of extra time. The incredible campaign was also notable as Chris Waddle was voted the football writers' player of the season, the first and only time this accolade has been bestowed on a Wednesday player.

Despite failing to secure a trophy, the Owls were again among the favourites for the title with a club record £2.75 million transfer fee paid twice to secure the services of England internationals Des Walker and Andy Sinton. The protracted club record £3 million sale of Paul Warhurst to big-spending Blackburn Rovers also took place, while Owls fans were flummoxed as their side failed to win or even score in the opening four games of the season! Thankfully, their favourites did return to form, but it was not enough for the expected title challenge, the Owls ending the season in seventh spot after finishing the season with a nine-game unbeaten run. The club also reached the semi-finals of the League Cup, but Manchester United exacted revenge for 1991 by earning a Wembley place with an emphatic 5-1 aggregate success. In hindsight, the season would prove pivotal to the club's long-term fortunes in the top flight, as the summer saw the departure of key players Nigel Worthington, Roland Nilsson and Carlton Palmer. With John Sheridan also out of favour, Wednesday spent the majority of the following two seasons at the wrong end of the table. The 1994/95 campaign ended with the departure of Trevor Francis after the Owls won only three of their final fifteen games, including a club record 7-1 home thrashing by Nottingham Forest. The new man at the helm was former Tottenham Hotspur boss David Pleat, and while Wednesday and his old employers Luton Town haggled over compensation, it was left to the backroom staff to take the Owls to Switzerland after a late entry into the much maligned Intertoto Cup. A scratch side lost to FC Basel, but despite winning both home games in their group – both being played at Rotherham United's old Millmoor ground – the Owls bowed out after failing to win in Germany against Karlsruher. When Pleat did eventually take the reins, he brought Belgium international Marc Degryse and Welsh international Mark Pembridge to Hillsborough. The former proved a successful capture, but it would be another season of struggle for Wednesday as they failed to

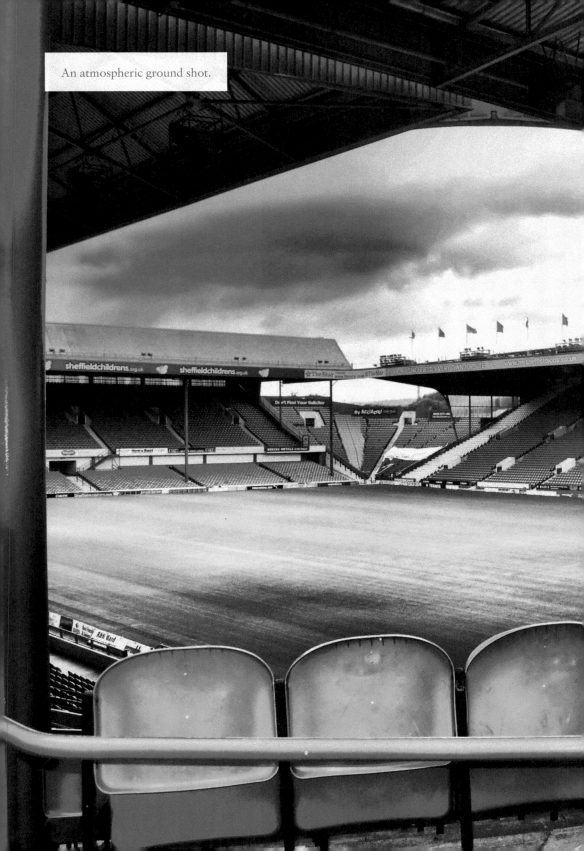

An atmospheric ground shot.

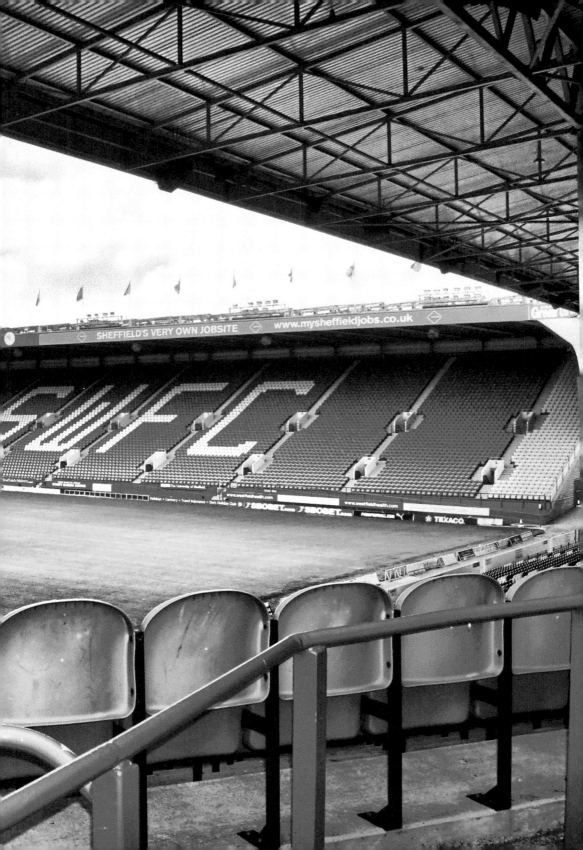

break into the divisional top ten and experienced a late flirt with relegation before securing their Premier League place with a final-day draw at West Ham United.

The season also saw a fee of £4.5 million paid to Red Star Belgrade for Yugoslavian internationals Darko Kovačević and Dejan Stefanović, with centre-forward Kovačević scoring twice on his full home debut against Bolton Wanderers on New Year's Day 1996. Neither player, though, made the impact that Pleat would have liked, and Wednesday collected a club record fee, which eventually rose to £4.6 million with add-ons, from Real Sociedad a few months later to end Kovačević's brief spell at Hillsborough.

After two seasons of struggle, the 1996/97 campaign saw a big improvement in Wednesday's fortunes as they made a terrific start, winning their first four matches to top the Premier League for the only time in their history. Although the Owls could not keep up that pace, they remained in the top ten places for the remainder of the season, with only a late loss of form dashing hopes of qualifying for Europe. The arrival of Italian Benito Carbone, for a club record £3 million fee, in October 1996 helped maintain good form in the Premier League, although the club was embarrassed in the League Cup as minnows Oxford United sent them tumbling out. A disappointing FA Cup quarter-final home defeat to Wimbledon ended dreams of Wembley, although the club's financial future looked rosier after London-based investment company Charterhouse Development Capital bought a 20 per cent stake in the club for the handsome sum of £17 million.

Part of the newly introduced funds probably went towards the club record £4.5 million signing of Paolo Di Canio in August 1997, with the newcomer quickly getting into hot water as he was fined by the FA for showing his buttocks after scoring at Wimbledon a few weeks later! Unfortunately, Pleat's new-look side failed to gel, and after losing 7-2 at Blackburn Rovers, the Owls quickly found themselves at the wrong end of the table. A 6-1 mauling at Manchester United marked the end of the manager's tenure at Hillsborough. Caretaker boss Peter Shreeves oversaw a remarkable 5-0 home win over Bolton Wanderers – all the goals being scored in the first half. Wednesday fans were then surprised to see Ron Atkinson back at the club after signing a contract until the end of the season. His impact was instant and three consecutive wins quickly pulled the Owls out of immediate danger. A crucial 3-1 win at Everton in April 1998 effectively ensured top-flight football for another season, although defeats in the final two games proved a sad ending for 'Big Ron' as club chairman Dave Richards announced the Owls would not be offering Atkinson another contract, and for the second time the two parties parted company somewhat acrimoniously.

In the weeks that followed, it looked likely that Glasgow Rangers boss Walter Smith would be the Owls' next manager, but after he had a change of heart it was former player Danny Wilson who was instead appointed to the role, moving from Barnsley. One of his first moves in the transfer market was the signing of Dutch international midfielder Wim Jonk, but within a few weeks of the season commencing he would lose the services of Di Canio, after the Italian famously pushed over referee Paul Alcock in a home game against Arsenal. A long ban, along with a £10,000 fine, put the popular Di Canio out of the first-team picture, and he would not play another game for the Owls – moving to West Ham United in a cut-price deal soon after his ban expired. New boss Wilson would oversee an encouraging debut season with the form of Benito Carbone, back at the club after refusing to be a substitute in a game at Southampton in August 1998, a key factor in a finish of just below mid-table.

GOODBYE TO PREMIER LEAGUE

The transfer dealings in 1999 would prove disastrous, both from a playing and a financial perspective, as Scotsmen Phil O'Donnell, Simon Donnelly and Phil Scott all arrived to great acclaim by the Owls, but also with extremely generous long-term contracts. Also arriving were Gilles De Bilde and Gerald Sibon, but sadly none of the five new men would make much of an impression on England's top division, and Wednesday fought all season against relegation, never moving out of the bottom three places. Early in the campaign, the Owls celebrated 100 years at their Hillsborough ground, but it would be a long and depressing season for Wednesday fans, with a shocking 8-0 defeat at Newcastle United – who were at that point bottom of the table – particularly difficult to swallow. The sale of Brazilian defender Emerson Thome weakened the ranks even further, with only the ever-dependable Des Walker and Swedish winger Niclas Alexandersson showing the form needed to launch an escape from the drop. Chairman Richards then resigned to take over at the Premier League, and it was new man at the helm Howard Culley who relieved Danny Wilson of his duties after Wednesday lost 1-0 to bottom club Watford. It was up to Peter Shreeves to take the role of caretaker manager once again, and results did improve, with Wednesday taking the fight until the last week of the season. The outcome looked set to be resolved on the final day, when the Owls led 3-1 with just over ten minutes remaining in a mid-week game at Arsenal, but the Gunners scored twice to send Wednesday tumbling out of the top division. With financial problems on the horizon and no manager, Wednesday went into the close season with the glory days of the early 1990s now just a distant memory.

STRUGGLES OF THE EARLY NOUGHTIES

The first job of the close season was to appoint a manager and, after the board survived a vote of no confidence at an extraordinary general meeting, it was former Bradford City boss Paul Jewell who was handed the task of getting the club back into the Premier League as soon as possible. Unfortunately, the new manager found his hands were virtually tied with regard to his ability to bring in new players, as the Owls' finances started to unravel following the unsuccessful fight against relegation. Some good news was the announcement of a £1 million sponsorship deal with Spanish lollipop makers Chupa Chups, but the club's playing squad looked somewhat threadbare as the new season opened with a draw at Wolves – Kevin Pressman being red carded after just thirteen seconds, setting an unwelcome record. With several of the club's big earners still on the treatment table, the Owls simply could not afford any replacements, and subsequently endured a terrible start, leaving fans to worry that Wednesday would get out of the division at the first time of asking but at the wrong end!

A club record run of eight consecutive League defeats saw an air of despondency settle around Hillsborough, and hopes of Charterhouse bailing the club out of their financial straitjacket ended when they cut ties with Wednesday in January 2001, after having written off the majority of their multi-million-pound investment – new Owls board member Dave Allen buying their remaining shares a few weeks later. It was inevitable that Jewell would not last the season and a heavy defeat at Wimbledon in February 2001 pushed Wednesday to the bottom of the First Division and spelt the end of a turbulent reign for the Liverpudlian. The same day also saw chairman Culley replaced by local businessman Geoff Hulley. One of Hulley's first acts was to announce the return of former coach Peter Shreeves as caretaker boss until the end of the season. The signing of Trond Soltvedt and the return of Carlton Palmer proved a master stroke from Shreeves, and he somehow coaxed eight wins from the final fifteen games of the campaign – six goals from Gerald Sibon contributing greatly. Despite losing exactly half of their forty-six League fixtures, Wednesday finished the season five points from the drop zone, and hopes were high that the late season revival could be taken into the 2001/02 campaign. After saving the club from back-to-back relegation, Shreeves was handed a two-year contract in May 2001, but sadly he would only remain in the job for thirteen more League games, resigning after a 2-1 home defeat to Preston North End in October 2001 left the Owls back in the relegation places. The terrible start to the season also included the sad loss of reserve centre-half Tom Staniforth, who died suddenly on a night out in York.

With problems on and off the pitch, the manager's chair at Hillsborough was somewhat of a poisoned chalice. It was then the turn of former Welsh international Terry Yorath to attempt a rescue mission. He duly fulfilled his initial remit of saving the Owls from the bottom three positions – Wednesday just escaping by a solitary point from third-bottom Crewe Alexandra – plus Owls fans had the considerable bonus of watching their side reach the semi-finals of the League Cup, knocking out Premier League Sunderland and Aston Villa en route. A wonder goal from Matt Hamshaw in the 4-0 home quarter-final win against Watford helped Wednesday into a last-four clash with top-flight Blackburn Rovers, but defeats in both legs meant no trip to Wembley as Rovers progressed 6-3 on aggregate. The following season saw the Owls again at the wrong end of the table, but this time there was no escape, and Chris Turner, who had replaced Yorath in November 2002, failed to stop the rot. The previous summer had seen the signing of Brentford top scorer Lloyd Owusu and, on loan from Chelsea, Leon Knight, but neither proved successful, scoring only a handful of goals between them as Wednesday slipped into the third tier for the first time since the dark days of the 1970s. The cost-cutting sale of top scorer Gerald Sibon in January 2003 certainly did not help the cause, and relegation was duly confirmed after Wednesday could only draw at Brighton's temporary Withdean home on Easter Monday 2003. Incredibly, a week after suffering relegation, the Owls registered an astonishing 7-2 win at Burnley – the biggest away League win in the club's history – but it was too little, too late, and another win, on the final day, was no consolation for the long-suffering Wednesday fans, their team finishing four points behind fourth-bottom Stoke City. Top scorer was Shefki Kuqi with just eight League goals – the lack of a proven goalscorer one of the main reasons why the Owls suffered a second relegation in just three years.

It was again time to clear the decks and Turner released several players, including big wage earners Donnelly and O'Donnell, before Wednesday started the season in fine form, winning 3-2 on the opening day in the scorching heat at Swindon Town. The early League tables featured

Wednesday in the top three positions, but that was as good as it got as the club endured a hugely disappointing season that ended in a final position of sixteenth, the second-worst finish in the club's long history. The only real bright spot was a run to the Northern final of the Football League Trophy, but this also ended in disappointment as the Owls flopped in the home leg and exited 3-0 on aggregate to Blackpool.

CARDIFF GLORY BUT BACK DOWN

It was at this point that Chris Turner took draconian action in an attempt to change the club's fortunes, releasing a total of thirteen senior players, including the likes of Alan Quinn, Leigh Bromby and Kevin Pressman. It would be their replacements – players such as Glenn Whelan, J. P. McGovern, Lee Bullen and Steve MacLean – that would finally end the club's downward spiral, although it would be bittersweet for Chris Turner as he was sacked after his newly assembled side made an unconvincing start to the season.

The summer of 2004 saw the story of Ken Bates' unsuccessful attempts to take over Wednesday dominate the headlines, but for once it would be events on the field that made the news as the Owls slowly climbed the table with new manager Paul Sturrock in charge. The loan signing of Southampton utility player Kenwyne Jones proved a master stroke, and his seven goals in as many games propelled his temporary teammates right into the promotion mix. The Trinidad & Tobago international made a scoring debut for Wednesday in a 4-0 win at Doncaster Rovers, where centre-forward MacLean became the first Owls player since John Sissons – Burnley in 1972 – to grab an away hat-trick in the League. The loss of top scorer MacLean to injury disrupted the closing weeks of the season, but with Chris Brunt in fine form the Owls remained in the top six, clinching a play-off spot after a dramatic last-minute winner at Hull City. A home defeat to Bristol City on the final day seemed virtually meaningless as, a few days later, a goal from McGovern earned Wednesday a 1-0 first-leg lead after almost 30,000 watched the first play-off game against Brentford. A place at Cardiff's Millennium Stadium (Wembley being rebuilt at the time) was subsequently secured after a memorable night at Griffin Park where goals from Lee Peacock and Brunt clinched a meeting with Hartlepool United in the Welsh capital. An unprecedented following of over 40,000 Wednesday fans travelled to support the club, and it proved a tense afternoon as a goal from McGovern was cancelled out, and with the clock ticking it looked like the season would end in disappointment as United led 2-1. However, the game then turned in an instant as Wednesday were awarded a penalty and Hartlepool were reduced to ten men following the award of the spot kick. It was left to substitute MacLean (who was surprisingly named on the bench after his season had seemingly been written off) to rather nervously drive home the penalty and swing the momentum firmly the Owls way. A terrific strike from Glenn Whelan, early in extra time, put the Owls 3-2 ahead, and in the final minute there was an unforgettable moment for teenage striker Drew Talbot as he raced clear and rounded the 'keeper before rolling the ball into the net. Cue unbridled celebrations both on and off the pitch before the party started in earnest after popular captain Lee Bullen lifted the play-off trophy.

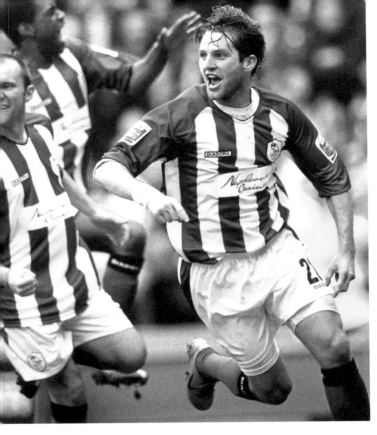

James Quinn celebrates a last-minute winner to clinch a play-off spot in 2005.

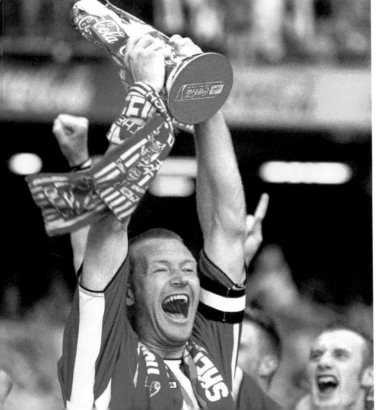

Captain Bullen with the play-off trophy

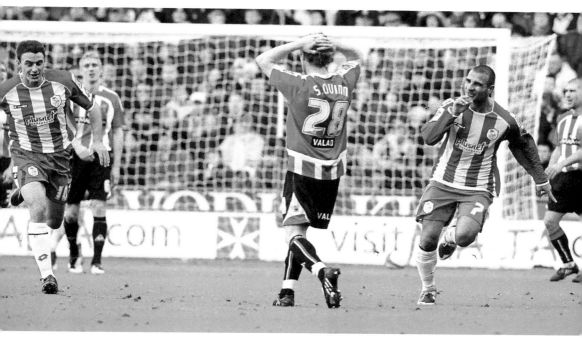

Above: Marcus Tudgay wheels away after his long-range effort clinched a double over United.

Below: Opening day of the 2010/11 season.

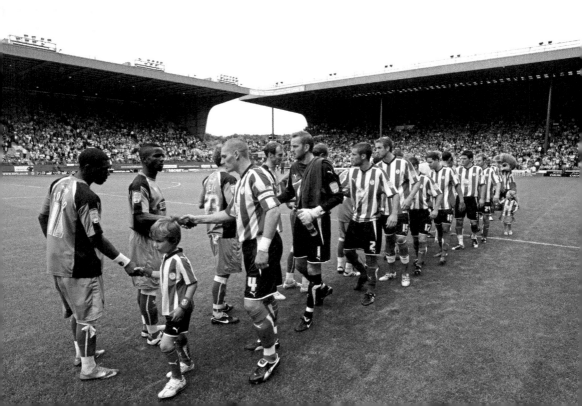

The two seasons that followed saw the club consolidate in the Championship before just falling short of a play-off place in 2007. The first season after promotion was marred by the pre-season leg fracture suffered by talisman forward MacLean, which kept him on the sidelines for the vast majority of the campaign, and a lack of firepower meant Wednesday spent the season at the wrong end of the table. A return to the scene of their relegation three years earlier – Brighton's Withdean Stadium – proved happier this time, as a crucial 2-0 win not only secured Championship football for the Owls but also relegated three other clubs, including the Seagulls. Despite Wednesday struggling at the wrong end of the table, crowds continued to rise at Hillsborough, with the Owls recording the highest average attendance outside of the top division. Further recruitment took place in the summer of 2006, with Madjid Bougherra being the headline capture, but despite Wednesday making a shaky start to the season it was still a major shock to Owls fans when popular manager Sturrock was sacked after the Owls lost 4-0 at Colchester United. Into the hot seat, on a temporary basis, came academy director Sean McAuley, and Wednesday duly picked up ten points from a possible twelve before new manager Brian Laws was appointed. The newfound form continued under Laws, with Mark Crossley, who later joined the Owls' coaching staff, becoming the only 'keeper to score for Wednesday in a competitive game when he headed home in the final minute of the December 2006 home match against Southampton. A run of five straight defeats checked progress, but another remarkable run drove the Owls to the fringes of the top six with only a loss at Birmingham City – in the last away fixture – extinguishing hopes of promotion back to the Premier League.

The summer of 2007 was dominated by the disastrous floods that hit the city of Sheffield, and Hillsborough was badly affected, with over £1 million worth of damage suffered to the ground as the River Don burst its banks. Owls fans were disappointed when Steve MacLean was allowed to leave for Cardiff City, while former Everton starlet Francis Jeffers checked into S6. After finishing in ninth place in the previous campaign, hopes were high of a promotion push, but the wheels fell off in spectacular style as the Owls set another unwanted club record by losing their first six League games of the season. The bad start was exacerbated by the departure of mercurial winger Chris Brunt to West Bromwich Albion for a sizeable fee, and thankfully came to an end when a goal from Jeffers secured a home victory over Hull City. An autumnal rally, fuelled by the goals of Akpo Sodje, pushed Wednesday briefly towards mid-table, but the terrible start would prove a millstone around the club's neck, and with just two games remaining they looked favourites to drop into League One. However, a vital 3-1 win at Leicester City followed, and a last-day survival was won as a sold-out Hillsborough watched Wednesday beat Norwich City 4-1 to preserve Championship status. The 2008/09 season proved to be quite uncommon for the Owls as Wednesday spent the majority of the campaign mid-table, being involved in neither the promotion nor relegation battles. The most notable event of the season came in February 2009 when a spectacular strike from Marcus Tudgay clinched the Owls' first double over the Blades for almost a century. The club also appointed a new chairman, with local businessman Lee Strafford filling the void left by Dave Allen's departure late in 2007.

The Owls made a reasonable start to Laws' second full season in charge, but there then followed a calamitous run of results that saw the side plummet down the table, dropping into the bottom three after a run of nine winless games. The loss of form almost inevitably led to the departure of Laws and the recruitment of former Preston North End manager Alan Irvine as his successor. The new man immediately triggered a run of three straight wins, commencing

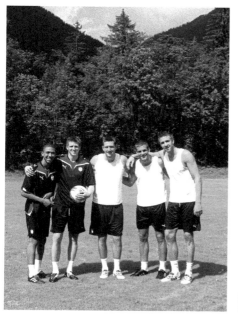 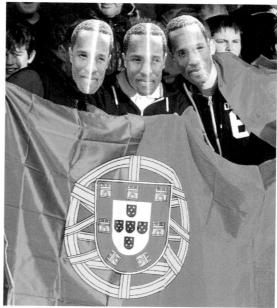

Above left: Pre-season in Austria – Palmer, Hinds, Boden, Spurr and Beevers.

Above right: You'll never beat ... Semedo day at Forest, November 2012.

Below: Contrasting emotions in the 2011 derby game across the city.

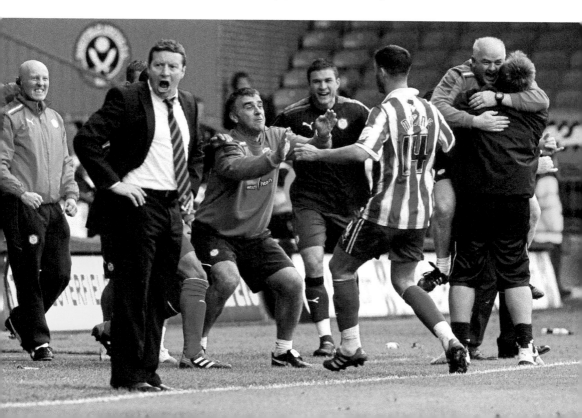

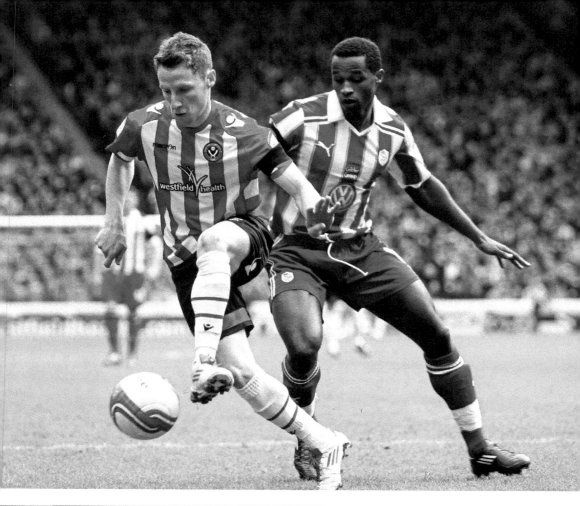

Above: Derby time, 2011/12.

Right: Reda Johnson celebrates the 2012 promotion.

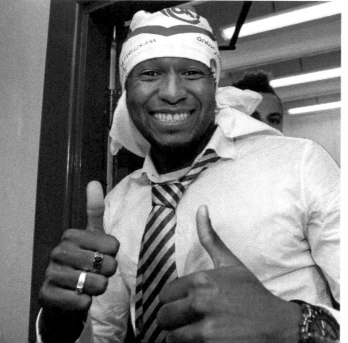

with a victory at Oakwell, but his influence waned and the Owls went into another last-day survival match against relegation rivals Crystal Palace at Hillsborough. Wednesday knew a victory would keep the club in the division, sending the London club down instead, but it was not to be. Despite goals from Leon Clarke and Darren Purse, the visitors earned the draw they required to dump the Owls back in League One, five years after securing promotion.

MILAN TO THE RESCUE

From both a playing and financial perspective, Wednesday dropping back into the third tier proved disastrous, as the Owls experienced a terrible season and their very existence came into question. On the playing front, Irvine recruited heavily, signing the likes of Neil Mellor, Giles Coke and Gary Teale, and Wednesday enjoyed a terrific start with a 5-0 win at Hartlepool United taking them top of the early League tables. A mini-slump followed, but as Christmas approached, the side moved steadily up the standings with a New Year promotion push a definite possibility.

Unfortunately, off the field events then started to engulf the club. The Owls' finances reached a critical point with Wednesday fending off a winding-up order after a tense day in court. This bought more time to find a saviour and it was at this point that former Portsmouth and Leicester City owner Milan Mandarić stepped into the breach with the Serbian-born US citizen becoming sole owner of Sheffield Wednesday and clearing the club's mounting debts. His first game in charge at Hillsborough provided a 'fairytale' 6-2 win over Bristol Rovers, but the remainder of the season was one to forget – the Owls careered down the table, with Irvine departing after a 5-3 defeat at Peterborough United in early February 2011. The appointment of former player Gary Megson proved a popular choice, and he presided over the remainder of the campaign as the club ended in a disappointing fifteenth position. Top scorer with twenty League and Cup goals, and player of the year, was the Neil Mellor, although his season-long loan meant he returned to parent club Preston North End when the season ended.

The new campaign opened with a home win over Rochdale, and 2011/12 proved to be one of the most exciting years in the club's history as the fight for promotion went down to the wire, with neighbours Sheffield United being central to the story. With loan signing Ben Marshall supplying the crosses, Gary Madine enjoyed a real purple patch in front of goal, netting eleven times in the opening thirteen League games as the Owls settled into a top three position. His final goal of the run was a dramatic late equaliser in the derby at Bramall Lane as Wednesday recovered from a two-goal deficit to secure a point that would prove hugely significant at the end of the season. Giant centre-half Rob Jones and Wolves loan player Danny Batth marshalled the Owls defence and, as the New Year dawned, it became obvious that the promotion places would go to Charlton Athletic, United, Wednesday or Huddersfield Town. A run of three losses in February hampered the Owls' progress and led to the dramatic, and unexpected, dismissal of manager Megson, despite Wednesday occupying third position. A manager-less Owls side then beat United 1-0 at Hillsborough before Dave Jones was brought in for the final thirteen games of the campaign. It would prove an incredible first few weeks for Jones as the Owls would remain unbeaten for the remainder of the season and, after an

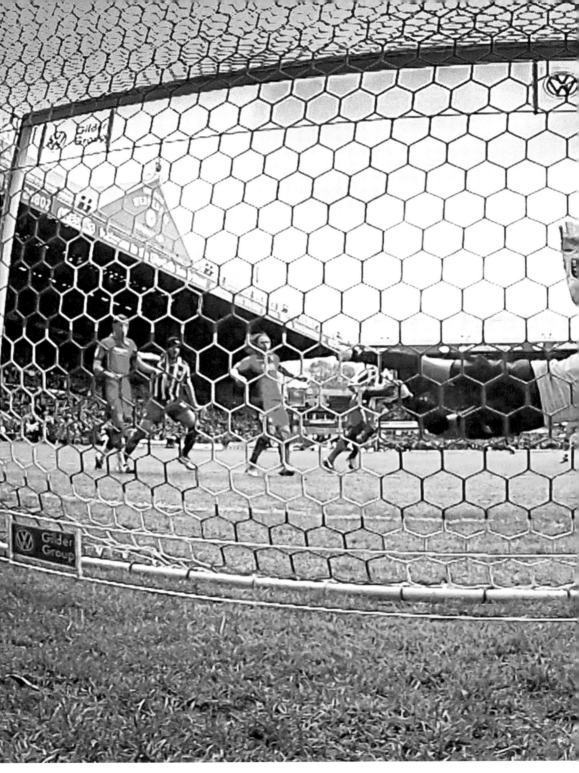

What a day – Wycombe, May 2012.

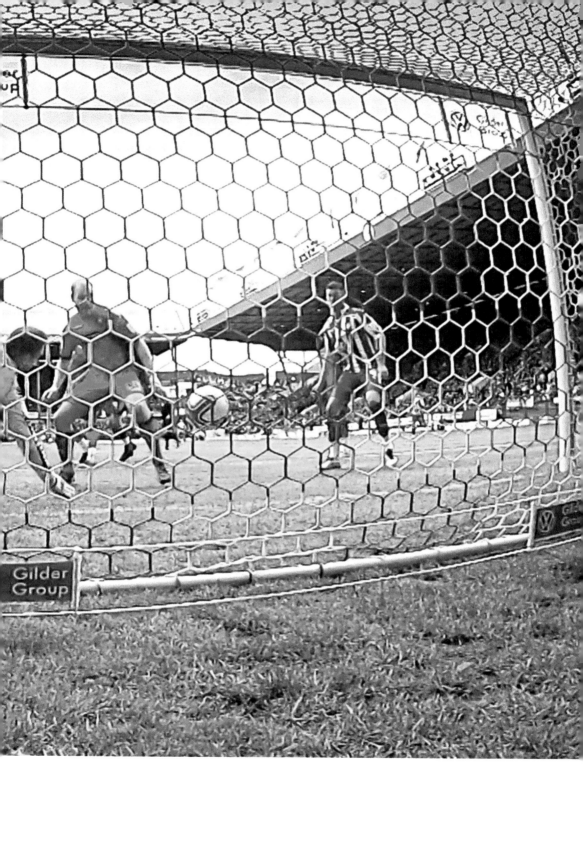

Easter Saturday win over Huddersfield Town, the fight for promotion became a three-horse race. Despite the run, it was still in the hands of Sheffield United for the runners-up spot – Charlton having streaked away at the summit – until two dramatic weekends swung the advantage firmly in favour of Wednesday. An injury-time winner for Wednesday coupled with a last-minute defeat for United suddenly narrowed the difference to a single point, and a week later the Owls won 2-1 at Brentford to go into second place, prior to the Blades' televised home game against Stevenage. The match was probably the most stressful ninety minutes of the whole season for Owls fans, as United recovered from two goals down to draw level but could not force a winner. The result meant Wednesday just needed to beat Wycombe Wanderers on the final day to clinch a return to the second tier. In front of a massive 38,082 crowd (the biggest outside of the Premier League that season) and with home fans uniquely on all four sides, Wednesday duly won 2-0, Michail Antonio and loan player Nile Ranger scoring, to trigger scenes of huge celebration at the final whistle.

The summer of 2012 was one of huge recruitment due to the increased demands of Championship football. With confidence high after the drama of the previous season, the Owls made a flying start, taking seven points from the first three games. New loan signing, from Barcelona, Rodri made a dream start by netting in the home win over Birmingham City, but it would be the only highlight for the young Spaniard as he failed to really settle and adapt to the 'rough and tumble' of English football. A tremendous run of nineteen unbeaten games – equalling a club record – ended at Crystal Palace, and Wednesday then went on a dismal winless run that did not see another three-point haul until early November. A televised win at Barnsley, though, proved a turning point, and the club experienced a vastly improved second half of the season, although they still needed to beat Middlesbrough on the final day to ensure survival.

The close season was relatively quiet with the likes of Stephen Bywater, Nejc Pečnik and Chris Lines all departing for new pastures while incomings included Jeremy Helan, on a permanent deal, Burton Albion winger Jacques Maghoma, defender Kamil Zayatte and former Austria Vienna forward Atdhe Nuhiu. Unfortunately, despite an encouraging performance in the opening-day loss at Queens Park Rangers, the Owls experienced a terrible start to the season and did not register a victory until the thirteenth League game, setting an unwanted club record in the process. The home win over Reading though proved somewhat of a false dawn and defeat at Blackpool on the final day of November spelt the end of Dave Jones' time in charge at Hillsborough. It was left to his assistant, Stuart Gray, to take temporary charge and he enjoyed a great start with Wednesday beating eventual champions Leicester City at Hillsborough. The appointment of Gray as permanent manager would follow several weeks later after a highly encouraging set of results had taken the club into the last sixteen of the FA Cup and out of the bottom three in the League – a 6-0 thrashing of Yorkshire rivals Leeds United being a definite highlight. Despite a disappointing FA Cup exit to Charlton, the revival in the League continued, and despite a late slump the Owls ended the season in a comfortable sixteenth place, two places higher than a year earlier but with five points less. The emergence of Kieran Lee, Chris Maguire and Liam Palmer as first team regulars gave Owls fans hope that Wednesday could yet become a competitive force in the Championship and one day secure a long-awaited return to the Premier League.

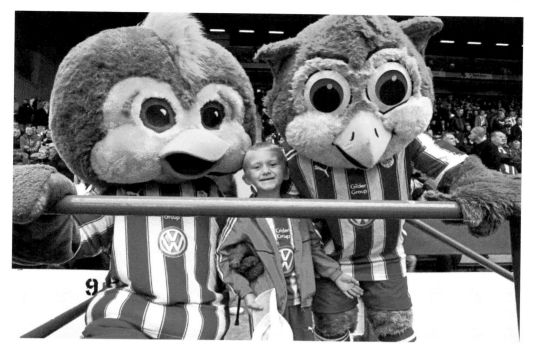

Ozzie and Ollie, 2012.

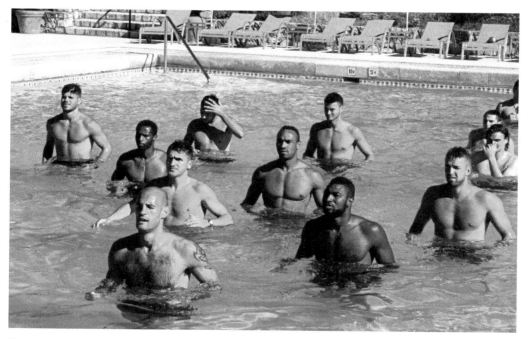

Pre-season in Portugal, 2012 – diamond formation!

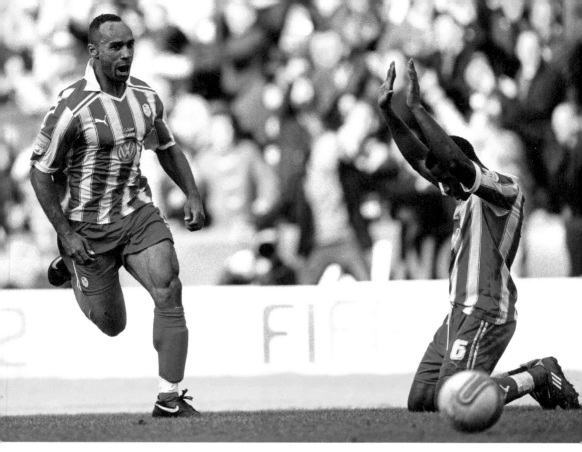

Above: Bow to the derby winner – O'Grady against United in 2012.

Below: Team group, 2013/14.

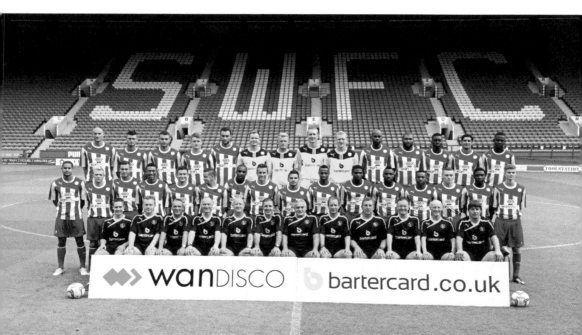